~~BUY THE BRAND~~

JOIN THE BRAND

IDEAPRESS
PUBLISHING

Published in the United States by IdeaPress Publishing.

IDEAPRESS PUBLISHING

ideapresspublishing.com

All trademarks are the property of their respective companies.

Cover Design by Hilary Clements

Layouts and Type Design by Lauren Knobloch

Production Design by Sara Klarfeld and Ron Baskin

ISBN: 978-1-940858-68-5   ISBN: 978-1-940858-30-2 (e-book)

PROUDLY PRINTED IN THE UNITED STATES OF AMERICA

By Selby Marketing Associates

SPECIAL SALES

IdeaPress Books are available at a special discount for bulk purchases for sales promotions and premiums, or for use in corporate training programs. Special editions, including personalized covers, custom forewords, corporate imprints and bonus content are also available. For more details, email *info@ideapresspublishing.com*.

HOW DOES YOUR BRAND BECOME A STICKER ON A LAPTOP?

Every brand is going after consumers who will love them. They are hoping to become a badge worn proudly, like a sticker on a laptop.

///

SOME ARE SUCCEEDING AT CREATING LONG-TERM BRAND LOYALTY AND OTHERS KEEP DIALING UP THE SAME TACTICS THEY'VE USED FOR YEARS.

Consumers are busy marketing themselves and give less than eight seconds to any message. No one wakes up every morning and decides to join a brand.

We've been feverishly studying beloved brands since 2013. Every year, we've asked thousands of people to tell us about their favorites.

This book breaks down all of the ways that people join brands, clubs or institutions that make them feel a sense of belonging.

As we studied consumers who interact with brands and then looked closely at joiners, we saw commonalities and broke them into a simple formula that you'll be able to use to create engagement and eventually brand fandom.

Above all, we looked at how and why they adopted one brand over all its competitors.

The first five years of research formed the foundation of our first book, *The Participation Game*. Participation, as we see it, is the X factor in brand marketing.

Continuing our analysis, we've started to see a progression from consumers who'd already joined a brand to consumers taking their degree of participation to another level—honest-to-goodness superfans forming brand communities.

BACK TO
THE WHITEBOARD

//

Two years ago, we called in our research team and asked:

WHO ARE THESE SUPERFANS?

WHAT TURNS A FAN INTO A SUPERFAN?

WHAT DRIVES THEM TO MAKE A CONSUMER BRAND SUCH AN IMPORTANT PART OF THEIR PERSONAL IDENTITY, EVEN TO THE POINT OF BANDING TOGETHER WITH FELLOW FANS?

WHAT CAN WE LEARN FROM THEIR JOURNEYS?

WHAT STEPS SHOULD MARKETERS TAKE TO ENCOURAGE LOYAL CONSUMERS TO FORM PASSIONATE BRAND COMMUNITIES?

We fielded six new studies on brand communities to determine how and why they form. The findings are here in this book, quantitative measures backed up with real life examples so you can easily absorb the insights.

Throughout, we've created some guidelines for building your own programs and, ultimately, communities.

It's brand affinity to the highest level.

Thanks for following along as we take you through it.

RESEARCH OVERVIEW

JOIN THE BRAND RESEARCH OVERVIEW
This book represents a culmination of six years of primary research conducted by our agency, Moosylvania, in partnership with marketing research firm, Great Questions, LLC.

We finished *The Participation Game* with anything but a conclusion in mind.

This led us to kick off a new round of studies to understand the power of brands that consistently drive participation and community formation.

2013-2018 FAVORITE BRAND QUANTITATIVE STUDIES
Each year, our baseline research starts with 1,000 U.S. consumers identifying their three favorite brands. Follow-up questions dig into brand relationships, loyalty and the role brands play in self-identification. The ultimate goal is to untangle the question: "When and where is the intersection between brand-initiated and fan-initiated engagement?"

2017 SUPERFANS VS. FANS QUANTITATIVE STUDY
We asked 250 brand fans and 250 brand superfans across the U.S. to tell us about the brand that has earned their greatest sense of kinship. The survey dug deep into brand communities and the sense of belonging within them.

2017 SUPERFAN ONE-ON-ONE TELEPHONE INTERVIEWS
Superfans were self-selected and defined as:

• People in my life know this brand is an important part of who
  I am, even if they don't get it. I love being connected to other
  people who are also fans of this brand, but you'd have a hard
  time finding someone who's as big a fan of this brand as I am.

Our interviews examined the roots of super fandom, the
personal experiences that influence them and where and
how they maintain connections.

GENERATION BY GENERATION LIFESTYLE ANALYSIS
In 2017, we utilized the customer insights software
platform, CubeYou and secondary research to identify five
of the most common lifestyle activities by generation. We then
evaluated the types of communities that each group joins on
their own based on their lifestyle and gender. This provides
a clear understanding of both opportunities and challenges
for marketers hoping to gain a share of their attention.

BRAND CASE STUDY EXAMPLES
Dozens of brand campaigns, communities, clubs, movements
and moments were studied to learn where relationships start,
build and ultimately empower consumers.

CMO SURVEY
In conjunction with Shopper Stories, we asked 100 CMOs how
they viewed their best fans and their ability to execute two-way
communication. Nearly all said they were doing just fine.

SMELLS LIKE MARKETING?

Before we look at joiners, we have to start with buyers.

///

STOP AND THINK ABOUT HOW YOU BUY ANYTHING.

You want to be in control and you want to make decisions based on your own tastes.

By its nature, promotion and advertising wants to exert control. It wants to influence the decision for the consumer. That's why, when done wrong, it's easy to turn people off.

Finding the right tone, getting the conversation going, convincing people to become consumers isn't easy and for many brands, the whole effort stinks. It smells like marketing a mile away. Potential fans can't flee the aroma fast enough.

As we ask consumers about their brand choices, we continue to identify brands that encourage connection without ever setting off the smell alarm.

Sure, these brand marketers are working hard behind the scenes, but from the point of view of consumers, it all looks natural, effortless. People find themselves wanting to connect and participate with the brand.

We'll look at how these odorless brands establish connection platforms and hold relevant, two-way conversations with consumers.

Once that's established, we'll explain how involved the average person already is with their existing interests and memberships. Busy people may not have the time to pay attention to your brand's message. But you can listen to theirs.

From there, we'll talk about building a "trust bank." Your brand or service has a currency and you can maximize it.

With these fundamentals out of the way, we'll move on to how your happy consumers become superfans. What makes them different from everyday fans? Where is the line drawn and how do you get more people to cross over it?

We've identified three steps to enticing consumers to **Join The Brand** by distilling best practices from those brands with a truly unforced marketing style:

IGNITE THE FIRE, FUEL THE FLAME + PASS THE TORCH.

Next, we'll discuss influence: the reason people change their mind and who influences them to do so. We'll show why paying people to influence others may never pay off. There's a breaking point, and we'll examine it.

We'll conclude by showing you that owning is better than renting. There are no shortcuts to loyalty.

Building genuine brand equity that rests in the mind of consumers and their spheres of influence will make you a force in the marketplace.

A force that doesn't smell.

03
PASS THE TORCH

ENLIST CONSUMERS

02
FUEL THE FLAME

UNITE CONSUMERS

01
IGNITE THE FIRE

ENGAGE CONSUMERS

TABLE OF
CONTENTS

CHAPTER ONE

THE EVOLUTION WAS TELEVISED

In *The Participation Game*, we identified that we are marketers marketing to marketers. Consumers are their own brands and our best bet is to build a rapport and support them.

Brands and consumers are inundated with messaging 24/7. Everyone is aware of the massive overdose of media, which is now made up of both brand and consumer-generated content.

This media overdose creates heightened competition to design the most shareworthy content, both for marketers and consumers.

The accessibility of media has shaped how we consume messaging, thereby changing what is entertaining to consumers. Longer form video used to make sense, but now with the smartphone's introduction in 2007, content has transformed to quick 10-second or less bites.

Let's look at three ways content has transformed over the last seven decades.

- **The original content creator**: Pat Weaver
- **The top ten list**: the copy that everyone can write
- **The original homemade content**: *America's Funniest Home Videos*

THE ORIGINAL CONTENT CREATOR

Sylvester "Pat" Weaver was a pioneer in both the entertainment and advertising industries, setting the tone for many of today's programming. As we produce content every day, we should pay homage to Mr. Weaver (father of the actress Sigourney Weaver). Among other things, Pat Weaver created *The Today Show*, *The Tonight Show*, *Wide Wide World*, and the variety format that eventually inspired *Saturday Night Live*.

Born in 1908, Weaver started in radio on the West Coast in the early 1930s when broadcasting was in its infancy. From the beginning, Weaver demonstrated his knack for captivating audiences. Starting in the late '30s, he promoted an on-air insult feud between comedians Fred Allen and Jack Benny that would go on into the early '40s to the amusement of millions of weekly listeners.

Originally, radio stations relied on advertisers to produce content in the form of one hour shows. Ad agencies created the concepts, hired the talent and paid the networks to air their shows. With this in mind, Weaver moved to the ad agency business in New York in the 1940s.

By the early 1950s, television began to gain momentum in American homes. TV networks were operating very much like their radio counterparts, by allowing ad agencies to create shows and promote individual brands.

Thanks to the expanding capability of the medium, budgets were exceeding $1 million per show and many advertisers couldn't afford to produce consistent content single-handedly. Weaver developed the idea of a network creating its own shows and breaking up the advertising into "magazines" of short commercials instead of advertising one brand with each show.

CBS turned him down, so Weaver brought the idea to NBC. It took two years, but even with resistance from the agencies, NBC started producing its own shows and selling 60-second spots. Weaver went on to serve as President of NBC twice in his legendary career.

Even after Weaver retired, he kept looking for what would come next, eventually becoming a pioneer in cable TV. He knew it would evolve. In his autobiography, *The Best Seat In The House*, he said, "The future of communications is so fascinating, I wish I had another lifetime to help it in realizing its potential."

Sylvester Weaver died in 2002.

> "
> The future of communications is so fascinating, I wish I had another lifetime to help it in realizing its potential."
>
> – SYLVESTER WEAVER

THE TOP TEN LIST

///

David Letterman has been off the air since 2015, but early in his career he set the tone for "top" lists forever.

Here's how it happened: one of Letterman's writers, Randy Cohen, was chatting with colleagues and brought up a funny Cosmo article with the title, "Ten Sexiest Men Over Sixty." Several months later, the Letterman version was introduced in September, 1984.

The title: "Top Ten Words That Almost Rhyme with Peas" was the very first one in a tradition that carried over between two networks, NBC and CBS.

The 'top ten lists' concept became a regular feature of the show and was shared with guest presenters and celebrities. The list became known for its drum-roll effect and reverse order format with the funniest answers loaded at the top to maintain interest.

When social content first became a medium, creators, such as Buzzfeed, started using these short, catchy lists that eventually caught on and became part of everyone's vernacular.

THE ORIGINAL HOMEMADE CONTENT

It was in the late '80s when another phenomenon gained traction—
video camcorders. These were big, bulky and cost $2,000, which was
the exact amount of the prize for winning with your funniest home video.

America's Funniest Home Videos ran originally as a special
in November of 1989. The series started in January of 1990 and is still
being produced today as the longest running primetime show on ABC.

The short form videos we know today on social platforms can all
trace their roots back to the original clips of dogs and kids doing
funny stuff. It all began with an ad in TV Guide magazine (another
relic) and asked viewers to send in their home VHS tapes.

Host Bob Saget would make faces and share blooper moments.
All together, they have produced over 650 episodes of short clips
in their 28 seasons so far.

In its first year, 32 million people tuned in. Each show featured
about 50 clips.

Ultimately, *America's Funniest Home Videos* demonstrated that
making videos is fun and gets the kind of attention everyone wants.

CHAPTER TWO

THE FALLACY OF ONE-WAY MESSAGING

///

Let's leave the past seventy years and fast forward to the present: Today, everyone is a smartphone content creator.

Messaging now falls into two buckets: one-way and two-way.

It's a simple equation: people want to connect with other people and brands can be a part of this fulfillment by acting like a friend.

Here are a few facts that our research uncovered which make the point:

- Consumers are on social media to connect with their friends, not brands.

- Word of mouth from friends and family is 2.5x more effective than TV, Facebook and YouTube advertising combined.

- Within consumers' top 100 favorite brands, ad spend can vary from minimal to massive and still achieve loyalty and popularity.

The information on page 25 articulates these points. Ultimately, personal connection is the gateway to fans and superfans.

Engagement is earned through relevant content that actually does something for people, something with value beyond the simple exchange of goods and services.

When we asked consumers why they were connecting on social media, only 3% said it was to connect with brands. Conversely, 55% responded they use social media to connect with their friends.

Connection platforms do their job when they deliver friends of friends to foster connection. Brands dig themselves into a hole if they can't deliver something of value, as well.

Smartphones enable consumers to continuously market themselves. And it goes everywhere with them. Their "buyers?" Their social circle. The better content people have to share, the more connection they receive.

Today, you're marketing to marketers. You'd win more if you became their friend.

55%

*Say the primary reason for using social media is connecting with friends.

Reconnection: 11%

Sharing photos: 8%

Reading posts: 6%

Getting up-to-date news: 5%

Viewing photos: 5%

Sharing information/posts: 4%

Seeking information: 3%

Viewing posts/photos from brands: 3%

Building my reputation: 2%

*Numbers may slightly exceed 100% due to rounding.
Source: 2016 Moosylvania Social Media Study

THE HIDDEN GEMS IN THE TOP 100

The list on page 28 shows the top 100 brands from an average of 18,000 consumer responses over six years.

We're constantly asking consumers about their favorite brands and compiling the results.

///

THIS IS NOT A LIST OF THE BIGGEST SPENDERS.
IT'S A LIST OF THE BIGGEST WINNERS.

Each year we continue to see that brands don't have to outspend to win.

Instead, they focus on connecting.

For example, have you ever heard of a company called Valve? They've been on our list every year.

Valve makes online games, a natural way for consumers to connect with each other, even share points with friends. As a brand, Valve puts their audience first.

How to Win Consumers' Hearts

MAKE THEM
LOOK GOOD

MAKE THEM
FEEL GOOD

KEEP THEM
ENTERTAINED

TOP 100 LIST* 2013-2018

1	Apple	19	American Eagle	38	Hollister
2	Nike	20	Disney	39	Converse
3	Target	21	Chevrolet	40	Sephora
4	Amazon	22	Kohl's	41	Costco
5	Samsung	23	Old Navy	42	Netflix
6	Sony	24	Under Armour	43	Gucci
7	Walmart	25	Express	44	Nordstrom
8	Microsoft	26	Macy's	45	Chick-fil-A
9	Coca-Cola	27	Toyota	46	Hershey's
10	Google	28	Honda	47	Kroger
11	Adidas	29	LG	48	Michael Kors
12	Nintendo	30	Hot Topic	49	BMW
13	Jordan	31	Gap	50	Levi's
14	Pepsi	32	McDonald's	51	PlayStation
15	Starbucks	33	Best Buy	52	Frito-Lay
16	Forever 21	34	H&M	53	Kellogg's/ Ralph Lauren
17	Victoria's Secret	35	GameStop		
18	Ford	36	Dr. Pepper/ Vans	55	Taco Bell

56 Dell

57 Chipotle/
HP

59 Mountain Dew

60 Nissan

61 Rue 21

62 Aéropostale

63 Bath &
Body Works

64 Kraft

65 Dodge

66 Coach

67 Trader Joe's

68 Asus

69 Ulta

70 Valve

71 Tesla

72 Ebay

73 Dove

74 J.Crew

75 Whole Foods
Market

76 Banana
Republic

77 Pink-Victoria's
Secret

78 Pizza Hut

79 Monster Energy

80 Subaru

81 Polo

82 Verizon

83 North Face

84 Puma

85 Marvel

86 Audi

87 Nestlé

88 Southwest Airlines

89 Wendy's

90 Jeep

91 JCPenney

92 REI

93 AT&T

94 Barnes & Noble

95 Guess

96 Mercedes-Benz

97 Ross

98 Tide

99 P&G

100 Carter's

*Based on 18,000 Millennial consumer write-in responses
(3,000 per year) 36, 53 and 57 exact ties. Olympic style ranking.

BIG SPENDER

Tide quadruples down on Super Bowl ads

//

During the 2018 Super Bowl, much fanfare was made about a four-part Tide commercial. It hooked viewers since it didn't start out as an ad for detergent. In fact, in each of the four spots, the advertiser was revealed later. Each ad was lauded as highly creative since the overall storyline was revealed in sequence with the game's four quarters.

The overall concept was a great example of "you know that we know that you know we're just making an ad here." So far so good.

However, the humor rested on the assumption that consumers watched all the ads from the beginning.

In the boardroom, of course, all four in sequence were brilliant. But if you missed the first one, the rest could be more puzzling than hilarious.

What else could viewers be doing at the time the first ad aired? Talking to a friend during a viewing party or at a bar? Visiting the buffet of chicken wings and nachos? Posting on social media?

Super Bowl TV spots don't command undivided attention anymore. And the days of asking the party to be quiet to watch the commercials are long gone.

About two years ago, Google started promoting the concept that with an attention span down to eight seconds, humans had less focus than goldfish. As Howard Tullman, from Chicago's 1871 incubator, likes to say, "Attention is the new currency."

At the very least, Tide's ad was an expensive way to get attention.

Tide spent $8.1 million for 67 million impressions. How many of those impressions were people who buy Tide? Certainly less than 100%. How many were actually engaging?

They got the mass right. What about the reach?

QUESTION

Let's give Tide the complete benefit of the doubt—just like the boardroom.

Leaving CPM constant and assuming 100% engagement, what do you think the efficiency of Tide's investment was in comparison to a digital buy?

- Equally as effective?
- Half as effective?
- One quarter as effective?
- One tenth as effective?
- One twentieth as effective?

$\longrightarrow$

ANSWER
To achieve the same number of
impressions on digital platforms,
where consumers were looking
while waiting for nachos, the cost
would have been $417 thousand.

So for one twentieth of what
they spent, Tide could have
had targeted impressions
with two-way potential.

———————

SUPER CLIO OR BEST DINOSAUR IN THE AD PARADE?

The ad community awarded Tide a "Super Clio" almost immediately.

But, The Drum magazine featured statistics from research firm Communicus. These stats said, after the previous Super Bowl, only 10% of consumers remember the average ad and know the brand advertised. Meaning that even though the ad was creative, was it successful? The report also went on to say that 80% of commercials during the game fail to change consumer opinion and intentions regarding a brand.

Transformation happens slowly, but the excitement and success around the Super Bowl highlighting Mr. Weaver's 1950s-era invention gets smaller every year. The hype used to be a month; now it's a week.

NOT SO
BIG SPENDER

On the other hand, take a brand like Kraft Mac & Cheese, targeting a similar demographic.

///

For Mother's Day 2017, the brand released an online ad that was built upon two-way communication. How did they do it? They started with a survey.

One thousand millennial parents took part in the survey revealing that 74% of mothers admitted to using profanity in front of their children.

Knowing this was the brand's core target, Kraft Mac & Cheese created a campaign around that statistic called "Swear Like a Mother." The digital video featured Melissa Mohr, the writer of *Holy Sh*t: A Brief History of Swearing*, speaking directly to fellow mothers and cheekily educating them on alternatives for the common curse word. The campaign was complemented by branded earplugs and Mother's Day cards.

Ultimately, the spot was a celebration of the hard work mothers do and recognition by the brand that all styles of parenting should be celebrated.

When we asked Eduardo Luz, Kraft Heinz's President of Grocery, how the idea evolved, Luz said they spent "significant time articulating [the brand's] purpose and human truths." Then, when deciding how to execute, they chose to avoid traditional media, like TV, because the brand was not seeing "real engagement on one-way channels."

Instead, they opted for social because it had the ability to "bring to life something that would be real, funny and that could spark engagement and conversation." And, considering that the original ad is still generating conversation and activity over a year later, it proves that the two-way social angle was the right call.

The ad was insanely successful, garnering over 4.5 million views, 70 million impressions and 769,000 engagements (likes, comments and retweets) in its first nine days. In total, over 387 million impressions were logged worldwide and the campaign snagged a Clio.

Even more impressive was the fact that in the 12 months following the campaign Kraft Mac & Cheese saw an increase in household penetration while sales and market share increased.

Compare that to Tide's four-part commercial and it becomes obvious which method ultimately connects to consumers. TV's one-way constraint means that Tide's commercial wasn't speaking with consumers, but at them.

And, while Kraft Mac & Cheese never released the full cost of the campaign, it's a safe bet that the video was well under Tide's $8 million plus Super Bowl buy. According to Eduardo Luz, the investment was "not huge, as [they] basically produced the video and used minimal paid on social to get it started."

Remember, the biggest spenders aren't always the biggest winners.

THE PURCHASE FUNNEL

Two-way is the way to brand loyalty.

//

Let's take a look at the purchase funnel, on page 38, and see how consumers are finding new ways to move through the purchase cycle.

As we noticed with Tide, marketers can no longer rely only on one-way communication, which is shown on the left side of the funnel.

There are too many opportunities on the right side of the funnel that enable more authentic communication with your audience. Developing a strategy that moves from one-way to two-way is key to creating opportunities for brand participation.

THE PURCHASE

ONE-WAY COMMUNICATION ──────

Push

Traditional

TV

OOH

Radio

Print

Paid

Digital Ads, Banner,
Pre-Roll, Rich Media

Retargeting

Remarketing,
Content Marketing

Link Bait, Paid Social
Promoted

Native Content
YouTube, PPC Search

SOCIAL

AWARENESS ──────→ CONSIDERATION ──────

SOCIAL

TWO-WAY PARTICIPATION →

Gamification

Push Notifications

Opt-In

Contests

Website

Emails

Apps

SMS

Experiential

Co-Creation

Video

Ecommerce

Personalized Emails

Phone Calls

Retail Ambassadors

CONVERSION ——————→ LOYALTY

FUNNEL

THE LOYALTY AMPLIFIER: TWO-WAY CONVERSATIONS

Entering into the conversation like Kraft Mac & Cheese did, opens the friend circle.

//

Other brands solely find this connection through customer service and personalized emails.

Check out this response I received when I returned a pair of shoes to Zappos:

Thank you for contacting the Zappos.com Customer Loyalty Team. My name is Davey. I'm happy to help you!

I'm sorry those didn't work for you! It never hurts to try something new on occasion though! I hope that the replacement works out, it sounds like you have had positive experiences with them before.

I hope you have some great music in your life. I'm listening to some New Navy. They are a cool band from Australia!

Please let us know if there is anything else we can do for you. We're here 24/7. Have a wonderful day and keep on rocking!

This response addressed my needs in a friendly manner and even referenced my musical interests listed on my social profiles. In today's purchase funnel consumers expect to interact, buy services and products, share social content, play games and be rewarded for their loyalty. Ultimately, they'll share their goodwill with their friends, who will enter from an entirely different point in the funnel. More brand awareness will come from loyalty than from mass distribution.

The purchase funnel has been changed forever with the ability to recruit consumers as advocates who can engage at any time. It takes original ideas and a kind of magnetism for brands to get themselves invited to these conversations.

The purchase funnel has been changed forever with the ability to recruit consumers as advocates who can talk back at any time.

WHERE MILLENNIALS INTERACT VIA SMARTPHONE

//

The statistics on page 43 shows the importance of connecting through email and websites, both owned properties, within the funnel.

These numbers reflect millennial consumers and the differences between 2017 and 2018 when it comes to where they are connecting. Marketers can see the importance of remembering owned channels. Of course, brands must still grow their social friendships, but be aware that the user base on social platforms is always fluctuating. It's not owned by the brand.

FACEBOOK

	17-27	28-37
20 18	40%	33%
20 17	52%	48%

INSTAGRAM

17-27	28-37
33%	24%
33%	19%

TWITTER

16% 13%
28% 17%

YOUTUBE

23% 17%
22% 18%

EMAIL

18% 22%
17% 8%

PINTEREST

7% 6%
12% 11%

SNAPCHAT

24% 11%
20% 10%

BRAND WEBSITE

20% 25%
19% 20%

TEXT MESSAGE

9% 11%
9% 10%

PEOPLE'S TOP CHOICES FOR CUSTOMER CARE

In the midst of so many connection platforms, don't underestimate the value of conversation. The chart on page 45 shows how consumers prefer to interact with brands for service. Even though social is just over a third of their customer care preference, email, live chat and phone calls are powerful connection tools that should not be forgotten.

5.3%
STORE

16.1%
1-800
NUMBER

34.5%
SOCIAL
MEDIA

19.4%
EMAIL

24.7%
WEBSITE/
LIVE CHAT

Source: Sprout Social, 2016

TWO-WAY CONNECTION STARTS WITH THE TWO-WAY BRIEF

To develop two-way campaigns, the effort must start with a two-way mindset. We've developed a two-way brief system, but before filling it out, here are five keys of briefing to adopt.

//

01

CONTEXT IS EVERYTHING.

How often do we see briefs that describe the ideal consumer, in their world waiting for the product or service we're briefing about? When writing a brief avoid visualizing the audience out of context. There's a whole universe of other daily moments that matter, all capturing consumers' minds and wallets in realistic ways. Write about those, too.

02

HOW DO THEY REALLY SAY IT?

We all know when we see an ad that showcases an overly perfected ideal scenario. While communication like this may make it easier to tell the message you want to tell, it doesn't successfully sell the brand. People take part in hundreds of conversations a day. They know real from fake. Start by listening. Then see how you can naturally add meaningful conversation to their reality.

03

CONVERSATIONS BEFORE TACTICS.

Start a conversation and see where it leads you. The best ideas always seem to be a solution that ignored the obvious. Executing tactics without a strategy is never going to be artistic. Remember, you care about the outcome, not how it gets there.

04

PRESCRIBING MEDIA IS DANGEROUS.

In the two-way world, the goal is to both intercept and engage. Fresh ideas can always be amplified once the message hits home. Good content will be distributed on its own. Let the idea prescribe the media, not the other way around.

05

TARGETING INFLUENCERS IS AN OXYMORON.

Of course, you want to reach influencers. Everyone does. But you have to earn them first. There's a path, starting with adoption to fandom to superfandom that we'll explore later. Instant superfans are pretty rare.

THE TWO-WAY BRIEF

The two-way brief is a system that builds to two-way conversation. Four quadrants, culture, consumer, category and company act as pillars to evaluate the current marketplace and conversation. The brief template, on pages 50–53, includes end-goals within each pillar (i.e. incorporate culture or intercept your consumer) as well as thought provoking questions bucketed into two groups (conversation or current situation and relevancy).

Start in any quadrant and use the questions on pages 52 and 53 as thought-starters, utilizing the two-way brief as an information gathering guideline.

Once you begin to formulate answers, start to assess and analyze how the answers within each quadrant work together, always taking into consideration what the conversation and relevancy is to today and how your brand can be a part of it.

CULTURE

Understand what's
current. Think about
entertainment, customs,
technologies, politics,
institutions and
organizations past
and present.

COMPANY

Solidify and share stories,
icons, beliefs, missions,
goals, development,
partnerships, knowledge,
purpose and benefits.

UNDERSTAND + INCORPORATE

CURRENT SITUATION + CONVERSATION

RELEVANCY

TWO-WAY

LISTEN + ACTIVATE

TWO-WAY CONVERSATION

Kon-ver-sey-shuh n; Informal interchange of thoughts, information etc.

INTERCEPT + ENGAGE

CURRENT SITUATION + CONVERSATION

RELEVANCY

TWO-WAY

DISRUPT + DIFFERENTIATE

CONSUMER

Connect with their habits, behaviors, lifestage, relationships, identity, emotions, communities and experiences.

CATEGORY

Understand the conventions. Think about symbols, language, assumptions, norms, rules, regulations and cost.

CULTURE

CURRENT SITUATION + CONVERSATION

What movements are taking place in society?

What changes are or should be occurring?

What conversations are taking place on a larger scale?

RELEVANCY

Articulate how the current situation is relevant.

How can your brand impact or join the conversation?

How can your brand include your consumer in the messaging?

COMPANY

CURRENT SITUATION + CONVERSATION

What conversations are you currently having with your audience?

What is your audience saying to you?

RELEVANCY

What changes can you make to tone, topic or channel that would better include your audience in your brand?

What conversations, ideas or partnerships can you amplify?

UNDERSTAND + INCORPORATE

CURRENT SITUATION + CONVERSATION

RELEVANCY

TWO-WAY

LISTEN + ACTIVATE

CONSUMER

CURRENT SITUATION + CONVERSATION

What is your audience talking about and where are these conversations taking place?

What needs are being left unfulfilled?

RELEVANCY

What is your brand's contribution to your consumers' world and voice?

Is their an opportunity for your brand to provide solutions?

CATEGORY

CURRENT SITUATION + CONVERSATION

What messages have been and are currently being portrayed?

What positioning are other brands taking?

RELEVANCY

How can your brand stand out from the crowd?

What can your brand deliver, that others cannot?

CHAPTER THREE

PAINTING BY NUMBERS DOESN'T MAKE IT ART

Consumers seek inspiration and that comes from fresh thinking. When marketers repeat messaging or simply execute a list of tactics, lacking strategy and relevance, it feels like painting by numbers—unoriginal and disconnected.

GETTING TO THE HEART OF THE MATTER

The goal is to begin having two-way conversations with consumers in a genuine way with human connections that are real.

//

This begins by articulating a brand story with originality.

Here is where the breakdown occurs for most brands. An original story still has to resonate.

Consider the lost art of brand manifestos. A work of literary prose that serves as the benchmark for future work. A mission statement set to copy. There are dozens of white papers and PDFs on how to write one, and a book by John Grant, *The Brand Innovation Manifesto* is a good starting point.

His definition: A brand is a cluster of strategically chosen cultural ideas.

His point: Understand the eco-system from your side and the consumer side. Make sure the brand story is rooted in truth that will withstand the test of time.

If an audience connects with your brand's story then they will find a way to tell it for you. The connection platform changes but the root remains.

Once the story is good enough for your consumer to tell their friends, turn up the volume and start promoting, collaborating and co-creating with consumers. Ask them anything. Celebrate their ideas. Be the life of the party. Make them look good, feel good and entertain them.

With this level of reverberation, they'll share the brand's story and experiences with their friends. The outcome is more awareness, except now it will have the share effect: endorsement plus reach.

" A brand is a cluster of strategically chosen cultural ideas."

– JOHN GRANT

THE STORY HAS TO REVERBERATE

A well-formed idea or brand story keeps your brand grounded in truth. But, it needs to be powerful enough to move through a progression.

Once consumers embrace your brand purpose, they will share it. The mission is no longer solely owned by the brand, it's re-interpreted, supported and believed by consumers.

To get to that level, remember original ideas usually win.

MORE AWARENESS

CONSUMER TELLS THEIR FRIENDS

CONSCIOUS HUMAN CONNECTION

ARTICULATED WITH ORIGINALITY

BRAND STORY

TWO-WAY COMMUNICATION

COLLABORATION + CO-CREATION

BELIEVABILITY + LONG TERM EQUITY

THE ROLE OF BRANDS HAS CHANGED OVER THE YEARS

Harvard Business Review published an article by Mark Bonchek and Cara France that redefined the role that brands play in consumers' lives.

///

Originally, brands represented a mark. Think of the ranch and the branding iron. Later it moved to being a singular idea. Brands evolved to represent experiences and finally, relationships. This created an opportunity for a singular brand to play a larger, more impactful role in the life of the consumer.

The evolution:

BRAND = MARK
to
BRAND = SINGULAR IDEA
to
BRAND = EXPERIENCE
to
BRAND = RELATIONSHIP

Bonchek and France reference that traditional roles have changed and the move to friendship can be seen in the personification of flight attendants on Southwest to Lyft drivers who want you to sit in the front seat.

BRAND = FRIEND
to
BRAND = FUN FRIEND

From there, the types of friends can be delineated to hip or trusted or any role that fits the need state.

With this flexibility, you can now cross the line into friendship and decide what role the brand plays in consumers' lives.

A FEW WATCH OUTS

//

Storytelling can easily become paint by numbers:

FALLING FOR REPETITIVE CONCEPTS.
By definition, Google has the answers. Unfortunately, everyone gets the same ones. Malcolm Gladwell says, "[Google] is too good because it gives you the most searched for answers." Therefore—unoriginal by definition.

BEING TOO SPECIFIC IN THE DEFINITION OF PROGRAMS.
Prescribing which media channels to pursue or tactics to use will not allow for creativity.

DEFINING AN IDEA AND THEN LOOKING FOR ITS "DIGITAL EXTENSION."
Since 2007, everything can be digital so there is no such thing as an extension.

AND SOME SAGE ADVICE

According to the London-based Institute of Practitioners of Advertising, automation and the "always on mentality" have created a rapid-fire approach to the marketing business. Thoughtfulness and intuitive understanding of a consumer need is as short as the five second videos we are posting.

What can we do differently? The IPA report quoted one agency executive saying, "We just need to figure out what question the client should be asking." Most of the time the agency/tactical buying sprees are moving so fast that we are all caught up in the game.

Legendary marketer, Fernando Machado, Global CMO of Burger King, has an "open brief." He issues an open-ended one sentence brief and shares it with his teams and his agencies once a year. He spends the year open to any ideas that answer it.

In the end, it takes a bit of risk and originality to make unique ideas come to life.

And it's not painting by numbers.

CHAPTER FOUR

#IALREADY-BELONG

The two-way brief we completed in Chapter Two says go to the target first before setting your agenda.

As we began to look at communities, it occurred to us that consumers already have a lot of options when it comes to how they spend their time and what to join. The ones they choose offer an emotional connection.

Brands need to start a relationship to earn attention. This demands brands become personal.

Friendship is personal; a far cry from transactional.

Just like any relationship, it starts by learning what the other is interested in.

We took a deep dive to understand how consumers are connecting on their own.

We wanted to identify the ways consumers are belonging without brands first, so we could ultimately see where brands play a role in this picture.

THE HEART OF THE MASLOW HIERARCHY

///

Maslow states that humans have five basic needs that must be fulfilled to obtain self-actualization. It starts with physiological needs like food and water and then moves up the pyramid to safety.

Here's where it gets interesting. The third step is "belonging." In order to make it to esteem and eventually self-actualization, a human needs a sense of belonging.

Because the need to belong is an innate human necessity, incorporating it into a marketing strategy is critical for brands who want to find themselves their own inner circle.

Twenty years ago, our future consumers may have sought connection within community clubs, their neighborhoods, social organizations, religion or family.

But today, the way we interact with one another has changed. There is less face-to-face, more screen-to-screen. The need to belong is craved minute-by-minute and fed with more non-traditional options.

SELF-
ACTUALIZATION

ESTEEM

BELONGING

SAFETY

PHYSIOLOGICAL

CONNECTIONS ARE BEING SOUGHT IN NON-TRADITIONAL INSTITUTIONS, INCLUDING FACEBOOK AND BRAND COMMUNITIES.

– SC TIMERS/USA TODAY NETWORK, 2015

THE CONNECTION GAME HAS CHANGED

PREACHING TO THE DIGITAL CHOIR

33%

of Americans attend religious
services once a week

while

76%

of Americans religiously
check Facebook once a day.

Source: Pew Research, 2016

DEFINING COMMUNITIES

Welcome to the real-time world. The need to belong is pulling everyone into the vortex of connectivity.

//

According to Harvard Business Review, as people form their own communities and join others, three distinct types of communities emerge: the pool, the hub and the web.

We analyzed pools, hubs and webs that are taking place today. Consumers join each of them fluidly and the level of connection they deliver varies.

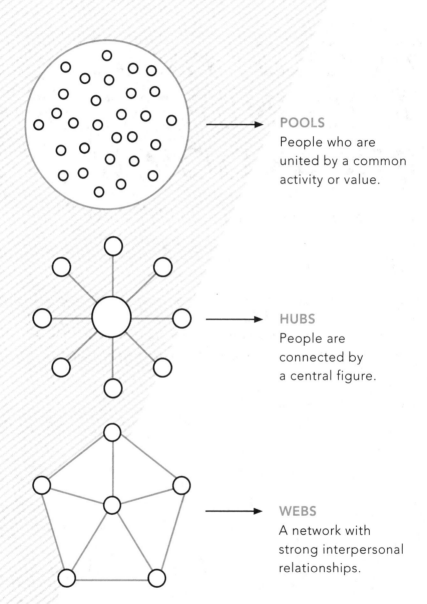

POOLS
People who are united by a common activity or value.

HUBS
People are connected by a central figure.

WEBS
A network with strong interpersonal relationships.

POOLS, HUBS AND WEBS: THE BREAKDOWN

These types of communities form naturally around anything from religion to office cultures to recreational sports.

//

But more fascinating, is that people are supplementing these traditional forms of communities with branded communities in the same way.

Let's look at some examples.

A POOL COMMUNITY

forms out of interest for a shared activity, value or passion point. Members gather around the action, but have less personal affiliation to one another.

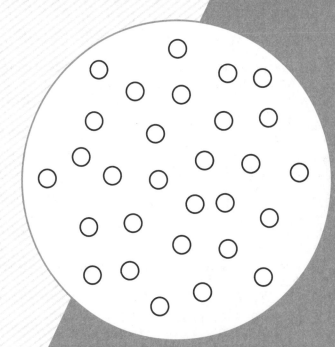

ANALYZING HQ TRIVIA: POOL COMMUNITY

HQ Trivia is an online trivia game currently played via a mobile app at 3 p.m. and 9 p.m. EST every day.

After creating an account, players are sent a push notification five minutes before each game starts. Once they log on, they join millions of other players in the HQ portal, where they interact on a message board until the game goes live.

After a series of 12 sudden death trivia questions, the remaining players split a pot of money that ranges depending on the day and time. By rallying around the shared activity of trivia, and the collective interest of winning money, a pool has formed.

Looking beyond the gameplay, there's a community here. The HQ community is virtual, based around a communal gaming experience.

However, the app has also crossed over into more traditional physical communities around the world. A few minutes before game play begins:

• Classrooms join the phenomenon by letting students play along.

• Offices have created company-wide calendar alerts.

• Families are planning mealtime around the game.

Beyond the group excitement, HQ has developed its own language. Players are affectionately known as "HQuties" and they understand the creative slang that the hosts speak in, like "Qumero, Numero, Uno" (code for "Question 1").

Aside from the literal cash that can be won, players trade referral codes for extra lives and are awarded with a live shout out on their birthdays or for winning.

Essentially, HQ is the first to successfully modernize the traditional game show. Creating a sensation that physically and digitally brings people together around the shared appreciation for anticipation, competition, entertainment and shared knowledge.

THE LESSON FOR BRANDS:
Find a collective passion point that consumers rally around. Develop ways to add value and nurture "pools" already in existence or initiate connection around individual activities.

HUB COMMUNITIES

Lady Gaga's
Little Monsters
28 million Instagram followers
56 million Facebook followers
Joanne world tour sells **841,935**
tickets

Gordon Ramsay
4.4 million Instagram followers
7.8 million Facebook followers
5.2 million fans tuned in to watch
the premier of his new show
24 Hours to Hell and Back

A HUB

shares admiration around a single individual.

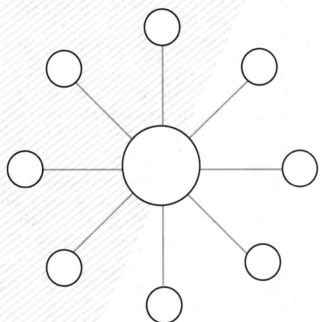

Like a pool, those in hubs join communities for a shared passion point and usually have weaker interpersonal relationships. However, in a hub, the shared passion surrounds a person, rather than an activity or interest.

BREAKING DOWN THE BEYHIVE: A HUB COMMUNITY

Beyond fame, Beyoncé is the quintessential leader of a 17,000+ active member fan-created hub. With thousands more who are less vocal, Beyoncé's BeyHive is more than a fan club. The online portal delivers Beyoncé-related content and is also a place where the singer can communicate with her fans directly.

Within the member-only community, fans discuss ways to promote the star's latest work and defend her against online trolls and negative media. Much like a traditional community, the BeyHive has a hierarchy and defined roles for each of its members.

Members call themselves "bees," and self-select the type of bee they resemble. For example, "worker bees" are dedicated fans who scour the internet for any bits of Beyoncé news.

They populate threads on the site with tips and sightings and perform deep research on any media site mentioning their idol's name.

"Honey bees" fit their name and save their energy for celebrating the singer on social media. Their counterpart, "killer bees" go on the attack to defend Beyoncé whenever adverse information or rumors are shared.

The bees live outside of the internet as well, showing up at concerts, providing sound bites for interviews and hosting podcasts and listening parties.

Hubs thrive off of enthusiasm surrounding a voice that cohesively feels larger than individual members' own, thereby defining a larger sense of understanding and self.

@BabyDollAriana

Follow ∨

Alright #beyhive Twitter do your thing! I got a
pair of tickets to #OTRII for Sep 11th in
Dallas, Tx that unfortunately I will not be able
to attend! They're really good seats! I paid
$430 for both and don't care to make a profit
just can't make it to the show!

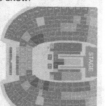

ROW
19

Laticia ™
@LaticiaD

#CarlosSantana after those #Beyonce is not a singer comments
7:27 PM - Feb 14, 2017

♡ 26   ⚲ See Laticia ™'s other Tweets

Tomi Lahren Feels the Wrath of the Beyhive After Criticizing Beyoncé

WEBS

are communities
centered around the
individual themselves.
They are personal.

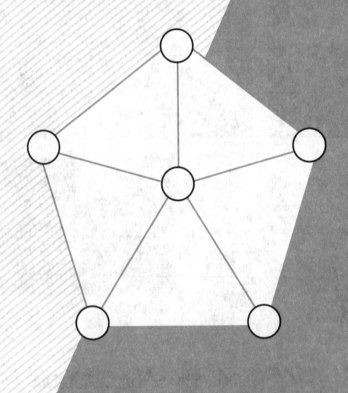

HBR: Getting Brand Communities Right—April 2009

Everyone has one. It's a connection of strong interpersonal relationships where the one-to-one connection is at the core of the community. This means the common interests across people are often relevant and personal.

Chances are you are a part of the 81% of Americans who have a social media profile. It's also safe to bet that you have multiple profiles, considering the average person has their name attached to an account on over seven platforms (Statista, 2017).

Consumers form multiple webs across multiple platforms. The immensity of each platform begs the question, if you have one profile, why do people need multiple webs? The answer: each platform has a separate form and function, allowing relationships to blossom in different ways.

For example:

- On Facebook (2 billion monthly users), the web is optimized around sharing personal life updates. Your connections are mostly family, close friends and prior classmates that live in messages, comments, groups and photos.

- On Youtube (1.5 billion monthly users), your personal web might be filled with fellow content creators and inspiring videographers who are all looking to share knowledge and creative talent.

- On LinkedIn (500 million monthly users), the orientation is career focused. Most connections are fellow employees, potential new employers and recruiters.

Whether virtual or in real life, webs still abide by a set of community standards. Interactions might be likes, shares, comments or conversation and language might have a professional or personal undertone. The one-to-one relationships that dictate these webs make them one of the strongest forms of community.

The opportunities are there. It's up to you whether your brand originates their own community or joins an existing pool, hub or web.

CONSUMER BEHAVIOR WITH THEIR FAVORITE BRANDS

At the end of the day, whether your brand fits into or champions a pool, hub or web, marketers still have to define how they support their consumer. That's the driving force.

We looked at how consumers are currently engaging with their favorite brands (see page 85) and noticed that a little over half say they purchase their favorite brand and over a third say they recommend it. Both behaviors marketers want to see. Both metrics that can still be increased. What happens if you are not a 'favorite' brand? After all, recommendation or word of mouth is king, so you have to figure out how to generate conversation.

We began to think about how both of these behaviors, purchase and recommendation, are ways that consumers support brands with money and with language. This means the brand/consumer "relationship" is mostly built on consumers bringing the brand into their world.

Looking at engagements that are built on brands supporting consumers (i.e. help them look good, feel good, entertain them) the numbers begin to dip. They dip even lower when looking at how successful brands have been in providing their audience with shareable content. Ultimately, we want to find balance in how consumers are engaging with brands. We see that consumers support the brands they love, but also that brands are actively supporting consumers' identities as well.

Consumers Believe Brands But, Still Don't

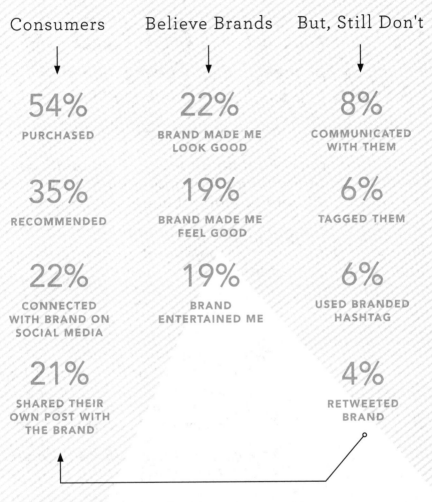

54%
PURCHASED

22%
BRAND MADE ME
LOOK GOOD

8%
COMMUNICATED
WITH THEM

35%
RECOMMENDED

19%
BRAND MADE ME
FEEL GOOD

6%
TAGGED THEM

22%
CONNECTED
WITH BRAND ON
SOCIAL MEDIA

19%
BRAND
ENTERTAINED ME

6%
USED BRANDED
HASHTAG

21%
SHARED THEIR
OWN POST WITH
THE BRAND

4%
RETWEETED
BRAND

Brands must create connection
in the everyday to establish an
emotional space long term.

FAN-INITIATED VS. BRAND-INITIATED

With so many opportunities to connect, brands need to solidify their everyday message. Without a consistent reason to engage, loyalty will fall through the cracks. And there are plenty of other brands waiting to take your place in line.

Ultimately, fandom should be a two-way street. Here are a few ideas to get you thinking (fan-initiated vs. brand-initiated).

FAN-INITIATED

29% of people share ideas/content/inspiration from a brand with friends.

27% of people showcase their fandom through appearance.

24% of people would attend a local event held by their favorite brand.

24% of people have included their favorite brand in a life moment/accomplishment.

21% of people know their favorite brand's "story."

BRAND-INITIATED

22% of people say that one or more of their favorite brands has a "story" that goes beyond its core product/services.

19% of people feel their favorite brand has a "way of life."

14% of people feel their favorite brands have a language.

12% of people have been invited into their favorite brands "network."

CHAPTER FIVE

COMMUNITY LOVE

Building a community means establishing credentials with consumers and that takes time and consistency. Consumer and brand values need to align. Think about REI inviting consumers to help clean up the outdoors. It fits with their identity.

Consumers are finding their interests and forming their own groups. Your brand can help provide a sense of belonging.

Brands have the
power to foster
a movement to
fulfill consumers'
need for belonging.

FIRST THEY JOIN A LIFESTYLE, THEN THEY JOIN A BRAND

In order to identify brand opportunities, we started with understanding what consumers are passionate about and where they want to engage.

//

We broke this down by generation to establish the top interest areas where each consumer group over-indexes. The diagrams, starting on page 93, outline these overarching lifestyle categories.

We took this a step further and developed generational lifestyle wheels to provide concrete examples of how each generation finds connection.

To build the model, we utilized:

• 2017 data from CubeYou, a customer insights software platform, powered by a representative panel of over 10 million American consumers' social data.

• Secondary research on each generation.

By identifying high-affinity categories across generations, we were able to outline lifestage commonalities.

This model allowed us to determine broad interest areas, and then build out the lifestyle wheels, starting on page 98, by diving into specific types of groups, clubs, memberships and communities that are commanding attention, time and money.

CATEGORY AFFINITY ACROSS GENERATION

$\longrightarrow$

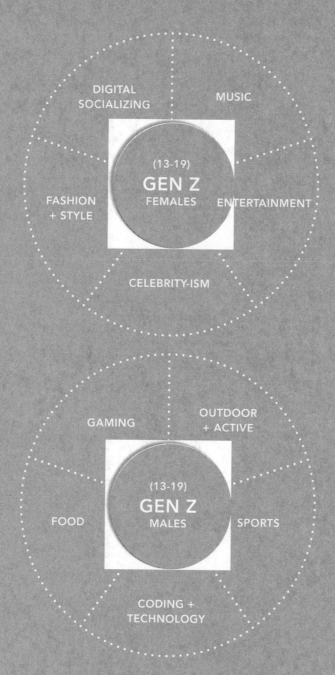

GENERATION Z
AGE: 13-19

DIGITAL SOCIALIZING

MUSIC

(13-19)
GEN Z
FEMALES

FASHION + STYLE

ENTERTAINMENT

CELEBRITY-ISM

GAMING

OUTDOOR + ACTIVE

(13-19)
GEN Z
MALES

FOOD

SPORTS

CODING + TECHNOLOGY

MILLENNIAL
AGE: 21-37

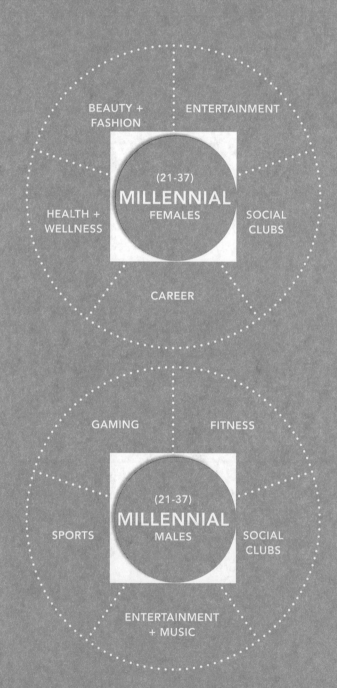

BEAUTY + FASHION

ENTERTAINMENT

(21-37)
MILLENNIAL
FEMALES

HEALTH + WELLNESS

SOCIAL CLUBS

CAREER

GAMING

FITNESS

(21-37)
MILLENNIAL
MALES

SPORTS

SOCIAL CLUBS

ENTERTAINMENT + MUSIC

GENERATION X
AGE: 38-58

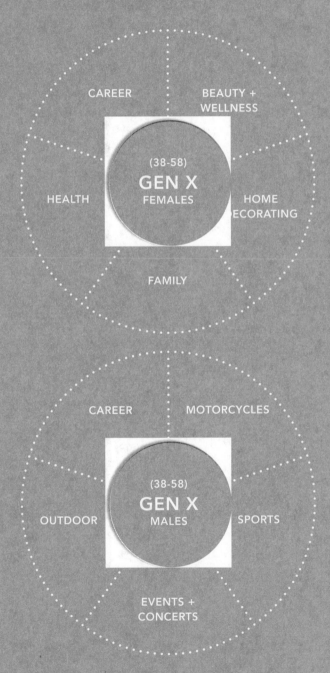

CAREER   BEAUTY +
WELLNESS

(38-58)
GEN X
FEMALES

HEALTH   HOME
DECORATING

FAMILY

CAREER   MOTORCYCLES

(38-58)
GEN X
MALES

OUTDOOR   SPORTS

EVENTS +
CONCERTS

BABY BOOMERS
AGE: 59+

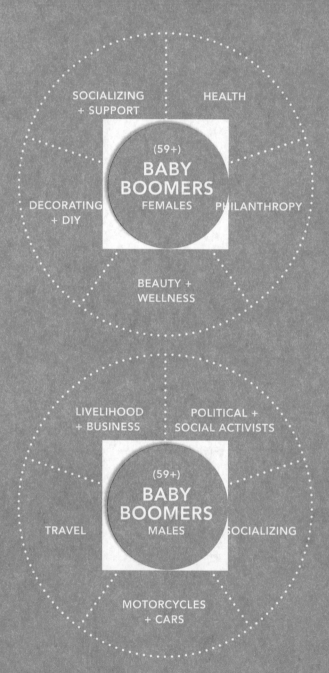

SOCIALIZING
+ SUPPORT

HEALTH

(59+)
**BABY
BOOMERS**
FEMALES

DECORATING
+ DIY

PHILANTHROPY

BEAUTY +
WELLNESS

LIVELIHOOD
+ BUSINESS

POLITICAL +
SOCIAL ACTIVISTS

(59+)
**BABY
BOOMERS**
MALES

TRAVEL

SOCIALIZING

MOTORCYCLES
+ CARS

FIND THE RELEVANCE. THEN FIND THE CONSUMER.

Each of the following lifestyle wheels provides a glimpse into how Generation Z, Millennials, Generation X and Baby Boomers self-identify through behavioral examples on an individual basis and within groups.

Utilize these wheels as a guideline. Think of a specific brand or the one you are supporting and then analyze where the authenticity of your brand and the reality of your audience overlap.

Pay most attention to understanding what consumers are already doing. Then think about where your brand can fit in.

Ultimately, you should create your own audience wheels to uncover specific behaviors and opportunities that are customized to your target's lifestyle.

DIGITAL SOCIALIZING
Obsessee

17K Facebook Fans
46K Instagram Followers

INSTAGRAM + FACEBOOK ARE HER
INNER CIRCLE CONNECTION POINTS

FASHION + STYLE
Ella Victoria

161K Subscribers

INSTAGRAM + PINTEREST FUEL
SHOPPING INSPIRATION

CELEBRITY-ISM
Shimmur

88 Countries
1.4K Fangirls

#SWIFTIES AS SOON AS
THE ALBUM RELEASES

MUSIC
Girls Rock!

Over 50 individual chapters/camps in the U.S.

CREATES AND SHARES HER
OWN CONTENT ON MUSICAL.LY

ENTERTAINMENT
Girl Cult

12.8K Instagram Followers

TEES + SWEATSHIRTS SHOW OFF
HER GIRL POWER

(13–19)
GEN Z

GAMING
The Art of Warfare

5K+ Members

STREAMING AND INTERACTING
WITH OTHER GAMES VIA
CAFFEINE, A SOCIAL
BROADCASTING PLATFORM

FOOD
Taco Bell

10.5MM Facebook
Followers

APPLYING FOR A LIVE MAS
SCHOLARSHIP #TACOBELL

CODING +
TECHNOLOGY
CoderDojo

38K participated in
dojos around the world

JOINING HIGH SCHOOL
HACK CLUBS

OUTDOOR + ACTIVE
Boy Scouts of America

2.3MM Scouts

WORKS HIS WAY TOWARD
EAGLE SCOUTS

SPORTS
Whistle Sports

1MM YouTube
Subscribers

70% OF BOYS PLAY ON
A HIGH SCHOOL SPORTS TEAM

Source: CubeYou+ 2017

BEAUTY + FASHION
Makeup Alley

700K Visitors a month

HAS CREATED AN INSTAGRAM
ACCOUNT TO SHARE MAKEUP TIPS

HEALTH + WELLNESS
Orangetheory Fitness

279K Facebook Fans

LISTENING TO HER FAVORITE
WELLNESS PODCAST

CAREER
FemCity

20K Facebook Fans

KEEPS AN ONLINE
PROFESSIONAL PORTFOLIO

ENTERTAINMENT
bRUNch Running

6.8K Facebook Fans

CO-COLLABORATES HER SPOTIFY
PLAYLIST WITH FRIENDS

SOCIAL CLUBS
Women Who Whiskey

6K Instagram
Followers

CRAFTING HER SIGNATURE
WEDDING COCKTAIL

(21-37)
MILLENNIAL
FEMALES

GAMING
Minecraft

11.8K Facebook Fans

XBOX GAMERTAG:
@APPSANDDESSERTS

SPORTS
Centennial 38

3.2K Facebook Fans

MEMBER OF "FAVRE DOLLAR
FOOTLONG" FANTASY TEAM

**ENTERTAINMENT
+ MUSIC**
Barstool Sports

1.2MM Facebook Fans

DRUMS IN A BAND

FITNESS
#Crossfit

38.6MM Instagram Tags

NEW FAVORITE PHRASE:
"WOD" WORKOUT OF THE DAY

SOCIAL CLUBS
Parlor

4.7K Instagram Followers

STANDARD PARLOR MEMBER

(21-37)
MILLENNIAL
MALES

Source: CubeYou+ 2017

CAREER
Lean In Circles

30K Circles
150 Countries

JOINING THE 4 MILLION PEOPLE
WHO MARCHED IN THE 2017
WOMEN'S MARCH

HEALTH
Weight Watchers

1.1MM Active
Members

CUSTOMIZES HER WORKOUT
ROUTINE WITH CLASSPASS

FAMILY
CafeMom

390K Facebook Fans
114K YouTube
Followers

SHARES MOTHERHOOD STORIES
ON INSTAGRAM

BEAUTY + WELLNESS
WMN Space

1.1K Instagram Followers

CONNECTS AND CONVERSES
ON THE MIDULT.COM

HOME DECORATING
HomeTalk

7.8MM Facebook Fans

BINGE WATCHING REPLAYS OF CHIP
AND JOANNA'S FIXER UPPER

(38–58)
GEN X
FEMALES

Source: CubeYou+ 2017

CAREER
Entrepreneur's
Organization (EO)

12K+ Business Owners
160 Chapters

WALL STREET JOURNAL PLAYS
A ROLE IN THEIR DAILY ROUTINE

OUTDOOR
Sierra Club

3MM Members
64 Chapters

FAMILY VACATIONS CENTER
AROUND OUTDOOR EXPLORATION

EVENTS + CONCERTS
Legacy Recordings

908K Facebook Fans

HEADING TO THE
LOCAL THEATERS

MOTORCYCLES
American Motorcyclists Association

1,200+ Individual Clubs/Chapters

PROUD OWNER OF AN INDIAN MOTORCYCLE

SPORTS
Fanduel

6MM Registered Users

PARTICIPATES IN ADULT REC LEAGUES

(38–58)

GEN X

MALES

Source: CubeYou+ 2017

SOCIALIZING + SUPPORT
Red Hat Society

135K Facebook Followers

JOINING THE 20TH
ANNIVERSARY BIRTHDAY CRUISE

DECORATING + DIY
Craftsy Unlimited

13MM Makers

HOSTING THEIR OWN
QUILTING AND CRAFTING CLUBS

BEAUTY + WELLNESS
Sixty and Me

500K Subscribers

FOLLOWING ALONG WITH
'EVERYTHING ZOOMER'

HEALTH
Silver Sneakers
14K+ Gym Partnerships

HIKING AND BIKING REGULARLY

PHILANTHROPY
Animal Rescue
1.3MM Followers

PARTICIPATING IN PAWS'
SENIORS FOR SENIORS

(59+)

BABY BOOMERS
FEMALES

HOW M
KNOW A
WOODST
OUR QUIZ
OUT!

Source: CubeYou+ 2017

LIVELIHOOD
+ BUSINESS
AARP

37MM+ Members

LOOKING TOWARD RETIREMENT

TRAVEL
Travel + Leisure

2.8MM Facebook
Followers

CROSSING ADVENTURES OFF
THEIR BUCKET LIST

MOTORCYCLES
+ CARS
Gold Wing Road
Riders Association

72K Members

JOINING WEEKEND 'RIDER GROUPS'

**POLITICAL +
SOCIAL ACTIVISTS**
Rotary Club

1.2MM Members

VOLUNTEERING WITH FRIENDS
AND FAMILIES

SOCIALIZING
PR!ME

984 Meetup Members

ATTENDING HAPPY HOURS, CONCERTS
AND PLAYS WITH PR!ME FRIENDS

(59+)

BABY BOOMERS
MALES

Source: CubeYou+ 2017

YOU CAN JOIN THEM BEFORE THEY JOIN YOU.

Supporting your audience instead of selling to them starts by understanding the communities they already form and join. This sets you up to recognize, with more authenticity, the spaces and partnerships that are in line with product, usage and greater brand mission.

///

Take Patagonia. They launched an initiative to take action in protecting public lands after the announcement that Bears Ears National Monument lost protection.

The movement was directly in line with their brand mission, which Patagonia CEO Rose Marcario, stated in her TIME article, "Protecting public lands is a core tenet of our mission and vitally important to our industry, and we feel we need to do everything in our power to protect this special place." (TIME, December 2017).

For many brands this type of radical activation is daunting and would get lost in the depths of approvals. However, Patagonia knew they could count on their consumer to stand by them because the movement affected the passion points of all outdoorsmen.

The activation gave voice to something consumers already cared about and created an even larger unspoken sense of belonging among anyone that dons Patagonia gear. It also brought their collective viewpoint to surface and created opportunities to physically join the mission to make a difference.

Are there partnerships that work toward a common goal for you? Activities you can be a part of within existing communities? How can you give a megaphone to what your audience is already saying?

THEY WANT TO JOIN BRANDS

OPPORTUNITY AWAITS

71%

said they want to represent
their favorite brand

24%

said they would join a brand
community if they learned about it

20%

said they are already part
of a brand community

TOP BRAND INTERACTIONS

Once the opportunities are established, the ideas start flooding in, but knowing how to activate is equally as important. We asked consumers how they have engaged with their favorite brands. Gaming and wearables ranked highest followed by online communities/clubs, reading brand fan stories and contests/promotions.

43%

GAMES

43%

WEARABLES (T-SHIRTS, HATS, PINS)

24%

ONLINE COMMUNITIES/CLUBS

22%

READING STORIES ABOUT OTHER BRAND FANS

20%

BRANDED CONTESTS/PROMOTIONS

16%

INTERACTING WITH INFLUENCERS WHO LIKE THE BRAND

12%

PLATFORM TO SHARE YOUR OPINION/VOICE

12%

REAL-LIFE COMMUNITIES/CLUBS

10%

CHARITY ACTIVITIES

4%

CO-CREATING PRODUCT OR SERVICE IDEAS WITH A BRAND

Source: Moosylvania Millennial Study, 2018

CREATE YOUR LIFESTYLE WHEEL

The following exercise helps you uncover the overlap between what your brand is saying and how consumers will best spend their time with you. That's where the real engagement begins.

OBJECTIVE
Extend brand experience; drive brand community.

JOIN THE BRAND STRATEGY
Your audience is already joining communities; identify where and how they fulfill their need to connect in order to support and activate against current behavior.

THOUGHT STARTERS
How can you think about where your brand and your audience overlap?

DEVELOP YOUR
BRAND WHEEL

WHAT DOES YOUR BRAND/SERVICE STAND FOR?

WHAT ARE NATURAL TOPICS FOR YOUR BRAND
TO CONNECT AROUND?

WHEN DO PEOPLE USE YOUR BRAND?

WHAT ARE TERRITORIES YOUR BRAND HASN'T PLAYED IN YET,
BUT MAKE SENSE TO ACTIVATE AGAINST?

UNCOVER
THE CONNECTION

CAN YOU PARTNER WITH A GROUP/BRAND?

HOW CAN YOU SUPPORT YOUR AUDIENCE'S
LIFESTYLE AND/OR PASSION POINTS?

IS THERE A MESSAGE THEY CARE ABOUT, THAT
YOUR BRAND CAN HELP GIVE VOICE TO?

WHERE IS YOUR AUDIENCE (MEDIA
CHANNELS, ACTIVITIES/EVENTS) THAT
YOU SHOULD BE PRESENT, TOO?

DEVELOP YOUR
AUDIENCE WHEEL

HOW DO THEY FILL THEIR TIME? WHAT ARE THEIR
PASSION POINTS?

WHERE ARE THEY GOING (PHYSICALLY AND DIGITALLY)?

WHAT BRANDS/SERVICES DO THEY CURRENTLY USE?

WHAT GROUPS/COMMUNITIES (BRANDED OR
UNBRANDED) DO THEY BELONG TO?

CHAPTER SIX

BUILD YOUR TRUST BANK

The more goodwill a brand generates, the more value it has.

The question becomes, how far can you take it?

In a popular TED Talk, Paul Kemp-Robertson noted that in any given day 30% of transactions at Starbucks are with Star Rewards. He goes on to say there are "more unredeemed air miles in circulation than there are dollar bills."

His point is that loyalty will become a micro-economy. The door is open for you to leverage that formula for your brand. What are people using your brand for? How can you make it better?

LOYALTY BECOMES A MICRO-ECONOMY

Consider the app Sweatcoin. Their tagline is, "the app that pays you to get fit." And, they deliver on that promise by literally trading sweat for redeemable points. Here's how the program works:

- The app tracks and verifies users steps.
- These steps are converted into Sweatcoin currency. 1,000 outdoor steps = 0.95 Sweatcoins.
- Sweatcoins are redeemable for valuable rewards, from PayPal cash, to trips, gear or donations.

Sweatcoin took a current behavior–consumers' desire to monitor physical activity–and turned it into a branded economy.

Another example of innovation within shopping was Nike's augmented reality lens promotion for the release of the Air Jordan III Tinker sneakers.

Jordan partnered with Snapchat, Shopify and Darkstore to create an experience exclusive to NBA All-Star Game attendees.

The experience? Users at the game found a special 3D AR lens that showed Michael Jordan, circa 1988. People could tap to see Jordan change into the current All-Star uniform, of course wearing the new kicks.

The reward? A QR code, powered by Shopify, was revealed. It allowed fans to buy the sneakers immediately and get them delivered in two hours.

Jordan created a physical retail opportunity where fans already were vs. simply telling them to look for the new shoes online in March.

The combination of digital connectivity and consumer involvement set up a whole new world of possibilities for building your brand's trust bank.

For consumers, complete loyalty or going 'all in' with any brand can mean amplified rewards. For instance, everyone can fly all year on Southwest and then shop the Southwest store at home or on the plane.

Southwest has successfully changed what was a transaction into a reward for a collection of experiences. In the Southwest example above, the first step is to fly for points. But the next step, where loyalty comes in, is when the brand asks, "What does flying do for you?"

Southwest acknowledges that people are flying to see people, go places and do things. The points they earn just make it better, they aren't 'the reason' to fly. Southwest happily brings this to life.

CURRENCY PAYS BACK

The overall concept behind branded currency is to enhance the user's lifestyle while solidifying the relationship. The more naturally the concept evolves, the more seamless it is for consumers to believe in the brand long term.

///

It's the same formula we've been dissecting: understand the lifestyle of the consumer and identify opportunities.

Just as every bank card had rewards until they reached parity, branded currency may go the same way. But in the meantime, it's still white space to be painted in with style and creativity.

BRANDS LEADING THE CONSUMER REWARDS PROGRAMS:

100+

MM MEMBERS

Amazon Prime | Nike+ | Walgreens Balance Rewards
IGH Marriott/Starwood | Ikea Family
American Airlines AAdvantage

92.2

MM MEMBERS

Costco

50+

MM MEMBERS

GameStop's PowerUp

20

MM MEMBERS

Emirates Skywards

12

MM MEMBERS

Starbucks Star Rewards
AMC Stubs

10+

MM MEMBERS

Beauty Insider by Sephora

5.5+

MM MEMBERS

REI Co-op

Source: See Works Cited

BUILD YOUR TRUST BANK

OBJECTIVE
Build value beyond the transaction.

JOIN THE BRAND STRATEGY
Develop your currency through quantifying and complementing behaviors that occur while people are using your brand/service.

THOUGHT STARTERS
Think about:

• How you can add value to the behaviors happening during consumption. (i.e. Southwest added greater value to flying, the behavior associated with the service, through trading points in for items/experiences.)

• Your brand currency, not just measuring behavior, but building onto an experience. (i.e. Fitbit not only measures the consumer's steps, it encourages more movement by enabling consumers to communicate and compete with each other.)

• What rewards or benefits could your brand provide consumers? Would items or experiences drive greater loyalty? What could consumers 'trade-in'?

• Does your currency come into play during the transaction or is it ongoing? (i.e. Starbucks consumers earn and redeem Star Rewards through purchase, but REI Co-op creates ownership through dividends each year.)

What category is your product/service in?

Are there other categories you can borrow from? (i.e. Southwest Airlines sells transportation, but rewards through tangible items and experiences.)

What does the moment of transaction look like?

Should your brand redeem and earn/pay with brand currency during the transaction?

What behaviors surround your product experience?

How can your brand create rewards around these moments? (i.e. If you sell spices, then your consumers may be cooking. Can you help them throughout the entire cooking experience start to finish?)

What can you provide to your consumer as a bonus or thank you?

Is there a simple and automatic way your brand can improve continuous engagement? (i.e. Spotify develops Daily Mixes for each listener—the more you listen the more custom these feel. The product is streaming music, the currency is automatic, customized playlists.)

SUPERFAN ME

//

As we've shown, communities play a role in fulfilling the need to belong. Brands have the opportunity to initiate these communities and camaraderie for their fans by rooting them in lifestyle and purpose.

But, to what extent do people participate in brand communities?

All communities have varying degrees of engagement across their members. Some members attach to the outcome of a product or the way a brand makes them feel. Others, known as superfans, self-identify through brands based on a set of beliefs, a way of life or values. Brand superfans participate in brand communities on an elevated level.

Our mission was to understand their DNA. How do superfans engage with brands differently? What are their favorite brands offering beyond belonging?

TALK THE TALK

Superfans are

4X

more likely to have regular dialogue
with their favorite brand

FRIENDS OF FRIENDS

Superfans are

2X

more likely to interact with other
brand fans on social media

YOU COMPLETE ME

Superfans are

2X

more likely to feel a sense of
belonging from their brand

SUPERFANS MOVE FROM PARTICIPATION TO IDENTIFICATION

Zoe Fraade-Blanar and Aaron M. Glazer, co-authors of *Superfandom,* define fandom as a verb: "We used to think that fans were people who liked something a lot, we now know that is not the case. Being a fan is active, it requires participating in a set of activities and showing you are more than just someone who likes something."

The notion that fans are active means superfans have a heightened level of participation. They are actually initiating brand activation and conversation.

In our research, superfans self-selected the definition: "People in my life know this brand is an important part of who I am, even if they 'don't get it.' I love being connected to other people who are also fans of this brand, but you'd have a hard time finding someone who's as big a fan as I am of this brand." This showcased that superfans celebrate their favorite brands not just as products but as personal identifiers.

Source: Moosylvania Superfan Study, 2017

Our research looked at behaviors to help identify when superfandom strikes and what the brand means to them on a larger scale.

We learned that more often than not, first impressions matter when it comes to fandom. It's more important than ever that all brand communication shifts from thinking product first to people first. In doing so, brands encourage and create fandom faster.

To make this shift, we learned superfans connect with brands that support:

• Communication: establishing a sense of connection and shared voice with fans

• Behavior: elevating a way of being or lifestyle

• Self-solidification: outward expression of their personality

FIRST IMPRESSIONS MATTER

76%
of superfans clearly remember the first time they tried the brand.

LOVE AT FIRST SIGHT

68%
of superfans knew the first time they tried the brand, they would return to it; a quarter can't remember a time they didn't love the brand.

IT CAN HAPPEN ANYWHERE

The initial introduction happens through self-discovery for **42%** and recommendation for **37%**.

THE WORLD OF FANDOM

Fandom takes place at varying levels—some fans dedicate their life to a brand, like those living in Disney's Celebration neighborhood, while others see the brand as an accessory to their day-to-day, think La Croix.

///

In his book, *Tribes*, Seth Godin explains "A true fan brings three friends with him to a John Mayer concert or to the opening of a Chuck Close exhibit. A true fan pays extra to own the first edition, or buys the hardcover, instead of just browsing around on the website. Most important, a true fan connects with other true fans and amplifies the noise the artist makes."

The point is that superfans wholeheartedly invite the brands they love into their world and brands must learn to do the same with their consumers. Superfans will propel the brand message forward and recruit other fans to participate for the sense of companionship in return.

Let's consider loyal sports fans. They devote seasons upon seasons to hoping 'we win.' They exhibit a sense of companionship through behavior.

For example, The University of Texas offers their knowing salute, 'Hook Em' Horns,' while The University of Alabama has their infamous chant, 'Rammer Jammer Yellow Hammer' and Wisconsin fans are proud of their 'Jump Around' tradition. Each of these behaviors serve as a way for fans to communicate with one another and showcase their pride.

Another example of expressing fandom comes to life when Comic-Con attendees participate in Cosplay. Fans champion characters they relate or aspire to by dressing up as them. These individuals identify with a character in the same way consumers identify with a brand and sports fans with a team.

Other fans simply want to celebrate their love for a product or franchise. Taco Bell knows this phenomenon well as a growing number of high school seniors want to have their pictures taken at the restaurant.

We asked superfans why fandom has become a larger part of their life. We learned: It's rooted in the product, but it lives in the intangible.

"

It looks good. It is durable and long lasting. The man behind the shoe is a freak of nature and I think I am too, and wearing Jordan's makes me feel like I am on that level."

– AIR JORDAN
SUPERFAN

"

"

It's something my mom and I bonded over every summer. As time went on, I was able to form relationships with people close to me because of the brand."

– LILLY PULITZER
SUPERFAN

It has made women empowerment important."

– UNDER ARMOUR
SUPERFAN

"

Socially and
politically active
in promoting
preservation of
the environment
and the lifestyle
the brand
promotes."

— REI
SUPERFAN

"

I've been a fan for as long as I can remember. It was love at first sight for me. It crosses boundaries—age, race, language... **"**

— DISNEY
SUPERFAN

LIVIN' LA VIDA LOCA

Celebration, Florida and Latitude Margaritaville in Daytona Beach, Florida and Hilton Head, South Carolina all take joining the brand to the next level.

Private clubs may have their own facilities, from Soho House to the American Legion Hall, but actually living within the brand is a reality in two Florida locations, and in another coming soon to South Carolina.

The first was Celebration, Florida, population 8,000. It was built originally in the '90s to be the city of the future, engineered by Disney and located near Orlando.

It's a storybook town, with houses that have matching shutters, specific varying colors and a quaint, small town feel. There's a steeple church, a school house and a town square, all functioning in perfect rhythm. Per its plan, Disney transferred ownership in 2004.

The appeal is the complete Disney experience with the opportunity to reside in a perfectly planned community. As one resident says, "It brings the simplicity of the past."

Meanwhile, across the state in Daytona Beach, a new retirement community is being planned for 55+ residents. The Jimmy Buffett-inspired community promises a Parrot Head lifestyle from the private beaches to mini-concerts.

These planned communities are promising the "laid back" feel of the Jimmy Buffett life. It's a chance to live the lines of the Buffett song, 'Changes in Latitudes, Changes in Attitudes.'

Homes are age-appropriate. Each is under 2,000 square feet with minimal groundskeeping required from residents. Model homes opened in February, 2018. The next development is also underway in Hilton Head, South Carolina.

Maslow would be proud: the entire hierarchy in one place!

GO AHEAD, STICKER YOUR LAPTOP

It's the ultimate connection. Becoming that sticker signifies that the consumer is all about your brand and your brand is all about the consumer.

///

We went on a mission to find the best examples of consumer connectivity and brand communities. We found hundreds of cases and began breaking them into common themes.

Our favorites are described on the following pages, under the formula we call, Join The Brand:

IGNITE THE FIRE, FUEL THE FLAME + PASS THE TORCH.

With an understanding of the ways consumers are wired, let's look at the formula as a filter and see what the best brands are doing.

JOIN THE
BRAND

CHAPTER EIGHT

IGNITE THE FIRE

///

Brands can be leaders with unique ideas. Brands with strong communities had one thing in common: a truly unique story that was clear and shareable. Each brand leveraged their story to start engaging their audience.

You will see that behind each story there is a sense of:

- Believablity
- Admirability
- Originality

IT STARTED WITH A T-SHIRT

One sure way to tell if your brand is resonating: Make a t-shirt. Will people wear it? Will they "badge" themselves with it?

///

When we get a new brand to work on, we'll often think about the filter: Do consumers love it enough to wear it? Why or why not? What has the brand tried? Can we make it even better?

This has led to complete marketing programs and long-term opportunities. You want to be the only sticker on their laptop, but you can start with being a regular in their t-shirt collection.

One of our deep dives early on explored entire companies that started with a t-shirt.

It goes to show that if they love the t-shirt, they'll love the brand. Turn the page to see examples of brands whose t-shirt propelled them to make it the nucleus of their business plan. (The only caveat is that the brand still has to deliver on what the t-shirt promises!)

IT STARTED
WITH A T-SHIRT

ICON IDOLATRY

UNIQUE STORY

IGNITE
THE FIRE

JOHNNY CUPCAKES

WHO DOESN'T LOVE CUPCAKES?

Observing his parents' long commutes to work sparked Johnny Earle's entrepreneurial spirit. He wanted to be able to do what he loved while also spending time with the people he loved. This resulted in him starting over a dozen businesses before the age of 16, including lemonade stands and manufacturing fleece scarves.

However, his break came later. After graduating high school, Johnny got a job at a record store and was awarded with a number of nicknames, one being "Johnny Cupcakes." He decided to print his new nickname on a t-shirt while processing another job order and soon everyone wanted one.

Johnny then began making more shirts, swapping out pop culture references with cupcakes. He began by selling them out of his trunk and on tour with his band.

The growing success of his side project soon prompted a life change. In 2004, he quit his day job and his band to pursue the Johnny Cupcakes retail concept full-time. He now tours around the country getting to know his consumers through pop-up shops, movie nights, dodgeball events and charity functions.

Because of Johnny's dedication to the brand and its consumers, a loyal and passionate fanbase has developed.

Currently 2,000+ people have the brand logo tattooed on their body while some superfans have more than 700 shirts in their collections. Fans have also been known to camp out for hours in front of the bakeries (the brand's term for "stores") waiting for the release of a new shirt.

Johnny Cupcakes shows that even a simple idea like a clever t-shirt can create community when a brand takes the time to understand its fanbase and spark two-way conversations.

FAT FACE

SELLING T-SHIRTS TO AVOID A DAY JOB

What is now a brand with over 220 stores spread throughout the United States, the United Kingdom and Ireland began on the ski slopes in France.

Tim Slade and Jules Leaver were looking for a way to fund their daily skiing adventures without having to be tied down to a desk job. To afford their lifestyle they bought t-shirts and sweatshirts wholesale and began printing designs on them themed around the mountains and ski resort. The original design was a shirt donning the line "Fat Face" which was a funny translation of the French Alp they called homebase.

They sold their creations to other skiers on the slopes and soon their brand took off. Their heritage is not lost on them today and they still operate with the same spirit and passion that established their name over 25 years ago. Today they sell to an international fanbase.

SERENGETEE

IT FIT FOR THEM

Serengetee started when two friends who were enrolled in Semester at Sea began visiting the local markets at their ports-of-call.

They found themselves collecting fabrics from countries in Africa, Asia and Central America. Upon their return, they wanted to use the fabric to give back to the communities they visited and connect people through a physical medium.

In 2012, they used every last cent and launched Serengetee from their dorm room. Now, they purchase fabric from over 25 countries and give back 10% of their profits to a number of causes that aim to improve lives in those communities.

Beyond the goodwill of the shirts, the brand has developed a community that is active on college campuses through ambassador programs and online using the hashtag #weartheworld, which has over 46,000 Instagram posts.

Serengetee's business model focused on connecting communities, both across the world and online, contributing more than what most would believe possible, all because of a t-shirt.

ICON IDOLATRY

Every brand has something that makes it feel permanent and bankable. From currency to bobbleheads, finding and exemplifying brand icons pays big in the long run.

//

The more consumers find badge value in the overall brand DNA, the easier it will be to build long-term relationships.

When you see an opportunity to bring any aspect of a brand's intrinsic or extrinsic characteristics to life, make it happen.

Do a laundry list and see what you stand for. You may just have an icon that can work a lot harder for you.

IT STARTED
WITH A T-SHIRT

ICON IDOLATRY

UNIQUE STORY

IGNITE
THE FIRE

FERNET-BRANCA COINS

KEEP IT IN YOUR POCKET

Fernet-Branca is a unique, $30 digestif/ liqueur. Fernet-Branca coins got their start in 2012 when a brand rep and his brother decided to revive the idea of the American military challenge coin. The idea behind the original coin was simple; a challenger asks you to produce your medallion and if you cannot, you're stuck with the bar tab.

If you have yours at that moment, your challenger has to pay the bill. The Fernet-Branca version follows similar rules but it also symbolizes much more. The coin acts as a secret handshake to get fans in the door of an exclusive club.

With coins only being released in batches of 100, the select few who hold one become members of a brotherhood comprised of top bartenders. Admission to this club is earned through exceptional craftsmanship and is considered the highest point in one's career, for most.

And, like any club, there are rules. While the secrecy surrounding the coin is in part what keeps the society alive, the members are expected to follow tradition. Bartenders must have the coin on them at all times and be able to produce the coin in less than four steps. Members must also never give their coin away, and if they do, they can only get a replacement from their original "bestower."

DISNEY PIN TRADING

BADGE OF MICKEY HONOR

Pin trading at Disney has been in effect since the start of the parks in the 1970s. However, it wasn't until a push from Disney at the turn of the millennium that made the pins the icon they are today.

Realizing their marketing campaign had turned into a hobby for many, they began celebrating park events with pin releases and holding annual pin events. By creating both readily available and rare pins as well as releasing ones for specific rides, days or events, Disney was able to strategically create demand which kept consumer interest high.

Additionally, the personalization aspect of collecting allowed fans to turn their hobby into a multi-year or lifetime project. Because each person was looking for a different pin to add to their collection, it meant that the trading, purchasing and searching would never stop.

Disney encourages fans to wear their pins proudly around the parks to open up opportunities for trading with others. "Hidden Mickey" pins, the most exclusive tradable ever released, are given to staff at parks and are available for trading. Those who wish to add one to their collection must engage with park staff to negotiate a swap.

Not only does Disney wisely keep momentum with the Hidden Mickey pins, but by making fans interact with one another and the brand, they are creating a deeper personal relationship that will, in turn, increase brand loyalty.

More than 60,000 pins have been created in the 17 official years of Disney Pin trading. Pins begin around $7 and can reach over $2,000 in auctions and private sales.

“
They have a convention every year and I've done that. They have a Facebook group, when I first moved to California, I didn't know anyone, so I became part of this Facebook group...the people...the camaraderie is kind of unique. We all have the same love, that's kind of cool. ”

— DISNEY SUPERFAN, 26

CHRISTIAN LOUBOUTIN

WEAR IT OUT

When Christian Louboutin borrowed an assistant's red nail polish and painted the soles of his shoes he had no idea that he was creating anything other than a unique pair of pumps.

Now, the iconic red soles do much more than identify high fashion, they show membership into an elite group of fashionistas that includes VIPs and celebrities in its ranks. Off of the red carpet, over 150,000 posts on Instagram are accompanied by #redsole and the brand's social pages total nearly 17 million followers.

Perhaps one of the greatest perks of being a loyal Louboutin fan is entrance to the annual sample sale. The exclusive sale is invite-only and never open to the public. The only way to snag an invite, aside from being an elite star, is to know someone on the inside.

In the case of Louboutin, the brand became iconic through their product itself, not a pin or coin. The brand used an ownable element of production, the red sole, and gave it the ability to be taken anywhere but still remain exclusive. In doing this, their product became an icon for the brand and a wearable "key" into a community of high-fashion consumers.

UNIQUE STORY

Your consumers need to care about your manifesto as much as you do.

///

The best stories are from the heart. They are typically built on something that really happened, or emerge out of the reason for the product's creation. In Adam Grant's book, *Originals*, he digs deep into the pragmatic effort most originators conjure up. There is always a method to the madness.

The easiest seed you can plant is your story. It's your why. We'll see from these examples that the more original the story, the more likely it will resonate with the consumer and also lead to a place that makes it impossible for other brands to duplicate.

Communities want to connect with a brand whose story they can believe in. Cognitive scientists like Michael Gazzaniga have proven that the brain organizes memory into plausible stories. Meaning the better and more believable the story is, the more memorable it will be.

Here are some examples of brands that truly amplify a unique story.

IT STARTED
WITH A T-SHIRT

ICON IDOLATRY

UNIQUE STORY

IGNITE
THE FIRE

TITO'S VODKA

THE DOG PEOPLE'S VODKA SPEAKS.
When Tito Beveridge started distilling his vodka, he had his dogs around throughout the trial and error process. It didn't take long for other dogs, strays included, to find a home at the original distillery. Always an animal lover, it became ingrained in the company mission to rescue each animal that crossed their path.

As the brand prospered, the company adopted the positioning line, "Vodka for Dog People."

Clearly, if you were to start your own distilled beverage, you wouldn't start with "What animal should you adopt?" This was original in every sense of the word and it caught on.

Go to Tito's site and look at the tab about their passion. It says, "the vision of our Vodka for Dog People program is to unite with our friends, fans and partners to better the lives of pets and their families far and wide."

"The program evolved organically," says Nicole Portwood, VP of Brand Marketing. "It grew out of our history of finding homes for the dogs that were left or wandered onto our distillery."

The idea of aligning a vodka brand with pet charities went on for 20 years before it naturally extended to a formal program with fan facing communication. Portwood said, "We're celebrating the animals that bring joy to our lives, and in the process, raising awareness and funds for the amazing organizations that make much of that possible."

One full-time member of the marketing team manages the Vodka for Dog People program. Portwood shared that there are 6,000 other charities they support, ranging from pets to arts and culture, medical to military and everything in between.

Currently, Vodka for Dog People has its own Instagram platform. It's the only place where the program lives independently but is very much a part of the overall story.

The brand's dedication is steadfast. "We will rise to the occasion no matter what this work brings! It's rewarding to support all of the incredible people who have dedicated their lives to making the world a better place for pets and their people, so we will keep doing what's needed of us in the space," Portwood says.

GUINNESS

WALK IN A VISITOR, LEAVE A FAN.

Ireland's famous stout was founded in what is now the brand's iconic storehouse, located in Dublin. Built in 1904 and acting as a fermenting plant until 1988, the building now hosts seven floors of rich history, interactive exhibits and dining options.

The unique brand story that is shared within the walls of the storehouse has turned the brand home into the most visited tourist attraction in all of Ireland. In the 17 years since the storehouse has opened, visits have continued to rise. In 2016 alone, over 1.6 million people paid $30 to see the attraction.

Notable points of interest that make this storehouse unique:

- The original building was signed over in a 9,000 year lease.

- By the end of the 1800s, it was the largest brewery in the world.

- The building architecture is designed as the world's largest pint glass (seven stories tall).

It's a complete "live the brand" experience from the moment up to 7,000 consumers a day walk in. The stories behind the brand are tangible and experiential, including a sample flight, impromptu Irish dancing and instruction on pouring the proper pint.

There isn't just a gift shop: it's a full-on retail experience spread over two levels. It's the perfect way to Join The Brand with something for everyone.

As a result, well over 100,000 posts on personal Instagram accounts have used #GuinnessStorehouse.

VANS:OFF THE WALL

#LIVINGOFFTHE WALL

HASHTAG FOR INDIVIDUALISM

Vans' connection to skateboard culture began in the '60s when skaters realized the sticky rubber soles were perfect for hanging on to the edge of boards. Feeling that they finally found a brand that understood them, skateboarders began visiting the Van Doren's shop frequently.

By asking for replacements of only the right shoe or extra padding in the back, a sort of organic evolution began as skaters and the brand grew up together. This resulted in collaborations with famous athletes like Tony Alva producing some of the most iconic models, like the "Era."

As times and trends changed, so did the brand and its collaborators. Along with this change, a mutual respect was born between Vans and skateboarders as they shaped the industry together. Even Vans' classic slogan, "Off the Wall" was derived from the early skateboarders who used to carve their way across empty swimming pools and pull aerials "off the walls" at the upper edge.

Today, their story is not lost on brand fans or the later generations who run the company. Still seeking input from skaters, Vans now sells more than just the perfect skateboarding shoe. Their "Off the Wall" slogan is now a lifestyle, encouraging consumers to be true individuals and unafraid to live differently.

Most importantly, fans are encouraged to share their videos no matter how they "live off the wall." Hit the hashtag and check it out.

//

ORGANIC VALLEY

UN-DOING THE CORPORATE WAY TO BE THE UN-CORPORATION

Organic Valley is a brand that began out of passion for the food we eat and the determination to do things the right way. In the '80s, when the agricultural industry told small Midwestern farms that they must switch to industrial chemical farming or "get out," one town took action.

George Siemon, a farmer in the La Crosse, WI region, rallied his town and called for change. Local farmers met at the courthouse and formed what would soon become the nation's largest farmer-owned cooperative.

Their mission was to change the way consumers thought about food and to produce organic food that protected the land, the animals, the economy and most importantly, human health. The guidelines they established ultimately helped to build the structure for the USDA's organic standards.

We're The Un-Corporation

Our farmers own the company. Not the other way around.
(That's why they're on the packaging!)

We're a cooperative of more than 2,000 small family farms.

In less than a year after its founding, the cooperative began to sell organic dairy milk. As the milk flew off the shelves, the brand grew to include other dairy products, vegetables, soy and eggs. Now, Organic Valley sells produce in all 50 states and had a record setting year with $1.1 billion in sales for 2016.

"Consumers, now more than ever, want to connect to their food. Because we are a farmer owned cooperative, which is as much a social mission as it is a business, we have values that are very different from most 'profit first' companies," says Marketing Director, Tripp Hughes. Ultimately, they aren't corporate and that appeals to many of today's organic consumers.

GOPRO

FOCUS ON THE MOMENT

Like some of the most iconic brands, GoPro also started out of a garage fueled by the passion of one person and a small amount of hard earned cash.

Nick Woodman, founder of GoPro, was surfing in Australia when he found inspiration for his newest project. He realized that extreme sports like surfing, skiing and mountain biking were being captured on cameras located far from the action.

There was no way in which a tripod on the beach or a jetski alongside a wave could capture the first person views of riding a barrel wave or landing a ski jump. From here, the GoPro was born.

Using his VW van as a rolling shop, Nick sold belts and beads until he had around $10,000 with which to invest in his new project. Through a long, laborious journey, GoPro has evolved to the company it is today, with over $1 billion in revenue.

The passion for capturing sporting adventures is what inspired the brand's roots back in 2002. It is still that same passion GoPro consumers feel each time they record their own footage and post it online.

Without these videos, GoPro may never have grown into the entity it is today. By staying true to their origin through messaging and quality products, GoPro is able to ensure that the foundation and values the company was built upon is still the story behind their success.

IGNITE THE FIRE

OBJECTIVE
Pique consumers' interest in your brand.

JOIN THE BRAND STRATEGY
Leverage brand leadership to capture consumer attention.

THOUGHT STARTERS
Think about:

• What is the key message your brand stands for? How can you bring your story to life? (i.e. Tito's Vodka takes what is ingrained in their brand heritage and activates against this with Vodka for Dog People.)

• Is there physical space your brand can 'own'? (i.e. Guinness' storehouse in Dublin, provides a tangible experience that lives on with consumers each time they buy the product.)

• Do you have an icon, how can you use it? (i.e. Disney's Hidden Mickey pins create an opportunity for consumer and brand personnel to interact.)

CHAPTER NINE

FUEL THE FLAME

Unite the believers with nicknames, common language and fan rituals.

Once consumers believe in the brand, they naturally want to develop in-the-know shortcuts.

Nicknames and unique slang find their way into the broader conversation. Think Natty Light instead of Natural Light or Micky D's instead of McDonald's.

Once believers start making their mark, it's your job to help them on their way.

CREATE A COMMON LANGUAGE

Songs have hooks–catchy phrases that are easy
to remember.

///

Brands can have them, too. When consumers start their own
nicknames and coin words or find expressions that the brand naturally
emotes, it's the beginning of a beautiful relationship.

Sometimes brands can get there by social listening other times it
takes a bit more inventing.

When nicknames evolve naturally, it's serendipity; other times they
just need a little help. It can be worth the time to create your own
naming conventions.

Listening can also be done the old fashioned way with qualitative
research with fans. Get them talking and find out if they have developed
verbal shortcuts to describe what they love about your brand.

Doing something special for "in the know" fans can lead to another
ritual, "the secret menu." Nothing makes people feel more special
than customized services.

Clearly, In-N-Out Burger could have told the first customer who asked
for something off the menu they couldn't do it. But they didn't and
the secret menu with its own code evolved.

Take a look at how you go above and beyond. Now see if it takes
you to a hook.

CREATE A COMMON LANGUAGE

CONSUMER CO-CREATION

GAMIFY YOURSELF

GOOD FOR THE SOUL

FUEL THE FLAME

IGNITE THE FIRE

ESSIE NAIL POLISH

pick your color

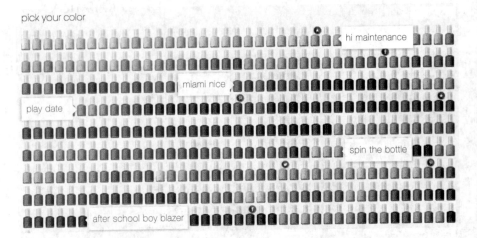

hi maintenance

miami nice

play date

spin the bottle

after school boy blazer

MIAMI NICE AND HI MAINTENANCE? SHINY SHARABLE MOMENTS FOR EVERYONE

Naming a nail polish isn't as straightforward as it sounds. What type of red is "red?" Is it cherry red? Pinot Noir red? How about the classy red solo cup red? Back when nail polishes were identified by a number no one had to think of such questions.

But, Essie Weingarten wanted to change that. The founder of Essie wanted to make picking out a nail color more personal and fun. As the first in the industry to give her polishes personality, she names each color for a memory, an inspiration or a motivating feeling.

Her polishes now come in shades like "barbados blue," "blushing bride," "on your mistletoes," and "using my maiden name." However, these sometimes pun-like, sometimes heart-warming names are more than just a creative expression.

For to-be brides, vacationers and party-goers these names are a guide. They help consumers sculpt a sense of identity especially when one of the colors becomes a signature. Queen Elizabeth is one such woman who has been wearing Essie's "ballet slippers" since 1989.

By creating these unique names, Essie not only helps women discover themselves, but it brings tribes together. Can your brand develop a set of naming conventions that allows consumers to describe themselves?

JEEP WAVE

TWO FINGERS SAY, "I BELONG."

For Jeep Wrangler owners, the "Jeep Wave" is a societal norm. The two-fingered gesture is an acknowledgement to fellow drivers of their superior choice in vehicle and a symbol of shared respect for the brand.

And, depending on which model year they drive and region they live in, there are differing customs. When driving with the top off, some Jeepers will extend their hands beyond the body of the vehicle while in the South, the wave might be replaced with a nod or a two finger lift off of the wheel.

Jeep fans have even gone so far as to assign a point system depending on the model number, as well as rules about who waves first and a calculator to help drivers determine their place in the Jeep hierarchy.

It is unclear where this mutual understanding began. Some believe it stems from a way of identifying friend vs. enemy during army transports while others say it was started by civilians once the Jeep became available to the public.

However, for the Jeep community, it doesn't seem to matter where the tradition started; what matters is that the community that has evolved continues the custom.

With a passion brand like Jeep, it is common to see membership rituals and customs appear. Because consumers already feel a heightened emotional connection to the brand, they are quick to acknowledge kinship amongst others who share their taste.

For Jeep drivers, this wave helps them recognize others like them, showing who is in their tribe and giving them a feeling of belonging. For the brand, it is a healthy sign that they are not just selling a product, but a lifestyle.

IN-N-OUT BURGER

IT'S FUN TO SPEAK IN-THE-KNOW IN-N-OUT LINGO

While many will claim the allure of In-N-Out is their never-frozen patties, veggie options and tangy sauces, there is another crowd who visits the chain because it allows them to belong.

In-N-Out's "not so secret menu" (it's posted on their website) allows consumers to order their traditional favorites with customizations in a way that sounds like slang.

For example, a "3x3" is just a cheeseburger but with three patties and three slices of cheese. An order of "animal style" equates to extra condiments and dressings while "protein style" swaps the bun for lettuce.

Even though the brand's unique lingo is not hard to learn or understand, it helps fans derive a sense of community and exclusiveness from the chain. Both employees and customers take great pride in the way orders are placed at In-N-Out and respect the tradition that the brand has created.

However, extreme enthusiasts have pushed even further and discovered that there are more secret menu items that aren't displayed on their "not-so-secret menu." As many as 29 options have been created along with many fan sites claiming to have found ways around the rules to customize orders even further.

CONSUMER CO-CREATION

Once you've made the transition from one-way to two-way, you are on your way to a new connection platform: co-creation. This can be simple—or it can be complex.

//

Asking consumers their opinion and responding on any channel is proof that a connection happened. Marketers can just ask consumers if they prefer A to B.

Cases in point include candy companies like M&M's that let consumers vote on a new color. They were making it anyway, consumers just get to participate.

Co-creation can take much more evolved forms with videos and memes and other types of content that serve the consumer as much as they serve the brand.

CREATE A COMMON
LANGUAGE

CONSUMER
CO-CREATION

GAMIFY YOURSELF

GOOD FOR THE SOUL

FUEL THE
FLAME

IGNITE
THE FIRE

AMERICAN EAGLE AE STUDIO

BUY YOUR JEANS AND WASH THEM, TOO

Proving they understand the millennial need state better than most, American Eagle opened a concept store, AE Studio, perfectly tailored for this generation. This isn't just a store, it's a co-created lifestyle experience located in Union Square in New York, adjacent to NYU's campus. Every inch is selling an experience, not just clothing.

iPads can be found along the denim wall, showing how each style and wash of jeans fits on a real person, as well as in the fitting rooms where shoppers can request help, order online and check out all from one location.

Keeping connectivity front and center, the brand's in-house social media team works directly out of the store in order to deepen two-way consumer communication and transparency.

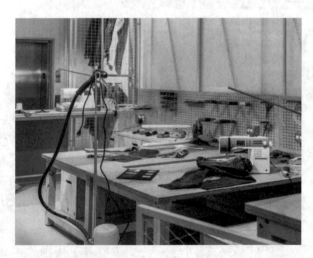

AE Studio also brings personalization to the consumer through a "Maker's Shop" in the back where alterations and customization through patches and leather tags can be added on-the-spot.

Perhaps the most millennial-friendly feature of the shop is the laundry and lounge area where local students can check off their mundane chores in an upbeat and exciting environment.

Sometimes co-creation can be about more than a single product. Asking your fans to help create their brand experience forges the way for a deeper and more personal relationship.

//

NIKE

ONE OF THE ORIGINATORS MAKES IT EASY

Almost everyone uses clothing and accessories to express personal style and identity.

Nike embraced it early on and launched their NIKEiD service in 1999. Nike's service allows consumers to customize clothing, shoes and accessories to match their style and needs. The price has actually come down in the past two decades with more technology and customer choices than ever.

Nike goes beyond the typical color choices and embroidered initials. Customers using NIKEiD can choose between dozens of parts of the shoe from the rubber soles to the stitching to be customized with colors, material types and text.

Nike has capitalized on their partnerships and made signature styles from athletes like Kevin Durant, Kobe Bryant and LeBron James available for personalization. The customization process not only draws traffic to their site/app and adds to the mentions online, but it allows for the brand and its fans to work together in person.

Consumers are given the ultimate experience to work one-on-one with Nike designers and choose from a broader range of products and personalization options at 102 retail studios throughout the world.

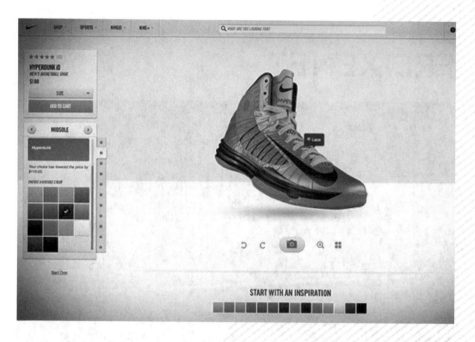

The NIKEiD service continues to grow as Nike adapts to the changing needs of its customers. New collaborations with celebrities, campaigns in Times Square, and design "battles" have kept Nike relevant and engaged in two-way relationships with their most dedicated fans.

FREIXENET

MESSAGE ON A BOTTLE

Freixenet's version of consumer co-creation comes not in the form of a personalized product, but instead, a customizable bottle. The brand's signature Cava comes bottled in matte black glass with a simple black and gold label: the perfect canvas for customization.

The brand encourages Cava lovers to grab a metallic marker and decorate the bottle to match any occasion. Their website hosts a tab with "DIY" bottle inspiration and their social media channels are filled with shots of creatively decorated bottles.

Aside from sharing UGC, Freixenet plays into the occasions aspect by running campaigns and activating partnerships. Around Halloween they celebrate "Cavaween" asking fans to "costumize" their bottles and place mini bottles at hairdressers so those getting Halloween hairdos can practice their decorating skills.

For Freixenet fans, any excuse to pop champagne is a chance to add a touch of customization to the party.

XBOX: DESIGN LAB

360°

YOU'RE IN CONTROL. NO REALLY.

Recognizing the growing need for consumers to have a voice in their purchases, Xbox gave fans the power to design the next set of Xbox controllers. Xbox Design Lab is Xbox's first attempt at online customization and it allows gamers to choose from a range of colors, materials and logos for their very own controller.

8 million ways to make it yours.
Xbox Design Lab

⊗ XBOX

#XboxE3

Fans can pick the finish and feel of each button and plate on the handheld to make it their own. A new partnership with the NFL and the addition of laser-engraved messages were added to the process this year, bringing the number of design possibilities to well over a million.

With gaming already an extremely personal virtual experience, Xbox was smart to bring a tactile element of customization into the gaming world.

JACK DANIEL'S:
BAR THAT JACK BUILT

A SUPERFAN WALKS INTO A BAR

Needing to solidify Jack Daniel's position in the spirits market and increase engagement amongst whiskey drinkers, Jack Daniel's used the namesake's birthday month as an opportunity to bring its fans together. Jack Daniel's led a social media campaign asking fans to help them build a bar to honor their founder.

Jack drinkers in Australia were asked to donate materials and time in exchange for whiskey. Pallets, paint, stone and lights began piling up at the build site and soon carpenters, artists and laborers followed.

The entire process was filmed and shared through social media to encourage other brand fans to leave their mark on the bar. After six weeks and $178,000 worth of donated supplies and time, Jack Daniel's unveiled the bar at a party held exclusively for everyone who had a part in its creation.

Ultimately the campaign totaled $84,500 in earned media and campaign engagement rose 263% from the previous year, all at the cost of 286 bottles of Jack. After the activation's success at multiple awards shows it was rolled out in other locations.

MY STARBUCKS IDEA

SERVING UP A LATTE SUGGESTIONS

My Starbucks Idea was launched in 2008 when the brand realized they needed to shift their focus to the needs and wants of their consumers. The site allowed consumers to suggest ideas, vote on other's submissions and learn about in-the-works projects. Once a fan submitted an idea, a team at Starbucks would evaluate the ideas for implementation.

The evaluation took into consideration the number of votes the submission received from other fans. It also looked at how unique the idea was and what the process would be to create it. By 2013, five years after its launch, Starbucks had fulfilled 277 of the 150,000+ ideas that were submitted through the site.

Here are some of the more well-known changes to the brand that originated as a My Starbucks Idea:

• Free wifi

• Splash sticks

• Cake pops

• Happy hour discounts

• Pumpkin Spice Latte

• Flavored K-Cup pods

• Mobile payment in drive through stores

• New flavors and menu additions

As Starbucks has evolved, so has the program. With millions of votes being cast and hundreds of thousands of comments, the brand was having a hard time sifting through the ideas and determining which were most pertinent. In 2016, Starbucks decided to close the forum and opt for a more simple submission portal that simply asks for consumers' ideas.

VICTORINOX SWISS ARMY: DESIGN CONTEST

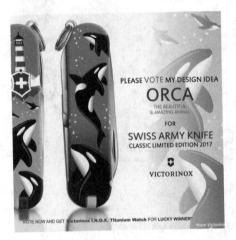

AVAILABLE IN RED OR WHATEVER YOU CAN IMAGINE

Sometimes the easiest way to learn about what consumers want is to ask the simplest of questions: If you could design a Swiss Army Knife, what would it look like? That open-ended simple question is exactly what Victorinox asked its fans when preparing to release its limited edition knife in 2012.

Hundreds of fans submitted their artwork and photos using the open innovation platform Jovoto. Six years later, Victorinox is still running the contest, using it to engage brand fans while building a community and sourcing new creations.

In 2017, the contest featured over 1,200 designs from participants in 69 countries. The ten winners were chosen by nearly 12,000 voters and received cash prizes as well as the chance to see their design for sale on the brand's site. Giving fans a real stake in the game and bragging rights? That's one great way to build loyalty.

SAPPORO 100:
BREWS YOU CAN USE

A WHOLE NEW TAKE ON BREW YOUR OWN
Sapporo has dozens of varieties in Japan and one way to expand their presence at shelf was to create a new SKU for fans, by fans.

The concept was to create a new brew with a taste profile that 100 users agreed upon, bringing a true meaning to its name. The company recruited the "tasting board of 100 consumers," and organized regular meetings to find the most satisfying taste profile.

The new brewers came from hundreds of miles away and were encouraged to share their adventures with friends as the project took six months to come to fruition.

GAMIFY YOURSELF

Under the credo of 'keep me entertained,' nothing gets more time on the clock than gaming.

//

Consumers will spend up to 20 minutes regularly playing a game, whether it's a contest of wits, skill or just amusement. There are two ways to look at gaming platforms. Brands can promote their one-way message during "contextually" relevant moments when consumers may be most susceptible. Or, they can choose to construct custom content that drives consumers to a purchase consideration or greater enjoyment of the brand's promise.

CREATE A COMMON
LANGUAGE

CONSUMER
CO-CREATION

GAMIFY YOURSELF

GOOD FOR THE SOUL

FUEL THE FLAME

IGNITE THE FIRE

MCDONALD'S MCRIB FINDER

NOTHING DRIVES VOLUME LIKE SCARCITY

The McDonald's McRib is a sandwich the chain releases only once each year for a limited time. The catch is that each individual restaurant decides if they are going to feature the item on their menu.

This in turn creates a craze amongst fans who not only want to get their hands on the tangy boneless pork entree, but make an event of finding the locations that serve the sandwich.

One fan even created a website, mcriblocator.com, where he tracked the sightings and allowed other fans to submit their findings. Seeing the potential for another brand touchpoint, McDonald's released their own app, the McDonald's McRib Finder, to help fans track down their favorite item.

The app works within iMessage, making it easy to share and drive buzz. Once in iMessage, consumers can pull up the app to see a map of their closest McDonald's and check to see if the location is selling the McRib. They are then prompted to send the location to their texting buddy in an invitation to splurge on the McRib experience together.

The app also comes with a set of McRib stickers to use when words are not enough. While the app is still only available to those on an iOS device it is a great example of a brand using a game-like experience to reach fans.

Even though McDonald's corporate does not control which individual franchises serve the sandwich, they are still able to create an entertaining and engaging brand experience.

CHIPOTLE: 'CADO CRUSHER

CHIP, DIP AND PLAY

Using games to reach fans and offer coupons is a tactic that Chipotle has perfected. 'Cado Crusher, one of the brands most well-known games was released ahead of the Super Bowl and in conjunction with Avocados from Mexico.

The game asked players to recreate the brand's guacamole in preparation for their "Big Game" party. The whack-a-mole style game primed fans with a list of ingredients to look out for and then filled their screen with the food items.

Clicking on an ingredient not found in the recipe like a football, tomato or tortilla chip resulted in a "fumble" or "offsides" penalty. Each of the three rounds increased in difficulty and fans were given timeouts peppered with brand facts in between.

At the completion of the game, fans were given a score, a title depicting their crushing mastery along with a mobile coupon redeemable for a free order of chips and guacamole.

All in, the game took less than three minutes to play and was easily sharable via social media and text messaging. This game was successful for many reasons:

- It was built as an HTML game.
- Consumers were not asked to download an app or deal with a slow loading time.
- The game was played within seconds of clicking the link using only finger tapping.
- It used timely and relevant national events to interest its audience.
- It was a perfect tie-in with the Super Bowl.
- The natural partner in Avocados from Mexico reinforced their quality.
- The reward, free food, was perfectly aligned.
- The game was sharable, enticing players to send it to their friends to redeem their own coupons. This helped to bring more people into the restaurant.

Look to Chipotle's other games to see more well-executed examples of the power of gaming.

UNDER ARMOUR: IT COMES FROM BELOW

THE GAME BEFORE THE GAME

Meeting fans where they already were was one of the factors that made Under Armour's "It Comes From Below Campaign" so successful. The sportswear brand used a game on Snapchat to elevate the sales of their C1N cleats and gear.

Using an avatar of Cam Newton, the Carolina Panthers' quarterback, players were asked to run through dark woods, dodging obstacles and pushing their limits further each time. The game was available through Snapchat ads as well as on Snapchat's Discover page.

The results were impressive. In the first day alone, 20% of Snapchat users played, spending on average 78 seconds with the game. And, 19% of those players shared the game with their friends.

Considering that at the time of release Snapchat had 158 million daily active users, Under Armour successfully reached a large portion of their millennial target.

Not only was Snapchat the perfect platform for the game, but Under Armour used an athletic figure relevant in their target's lives and a gameplay almost as simple as swiping through a Snapchat feed.

PATRON: THE PATRON EXPERIENCE

MAKING AGAVE AND GOOD STUFF

Adding gaming as an element of advertising can also come in the form of augmented reality. Patron used the software in September of 2017 to bring an added element of fun to the tequila buying experience.

Using the brand's app, consumers could virtually plant an agave farm outside their own hacienda that came equipped with a bar and bartender. While the players tended to their plantation, they could interact with the bartender who would introduce Patron's products. Tapping on the liquor bottles prompted the bartender to share the histories and tasting notes of each liquid.

Patron's activation mixed AR, gaming and education to deliver an interactive experience that generated fan buzz.

AUDI SANDBOX

PLAYING IN THE SANDBOX NEVER GETS OLD

Brands giving consumers a game to play has proven to be successful in capturing and entertaining fans. But, what if it could be taken one step further? What if instead of playing a game, the consumer was in the game? Audi did just that with an installation in their flagship Oslo location.

Audi asked fans to channel their inner child by playing in a sandbox. Consumers sculpted mounds, crafted tracks and designed an imaginary world. Audi then used

an infrared camera to scan the sand pit and create a three-dimensional version of the creation.

Taking it one step further, consumers were able to drive the very tracks they had just sculpted thanks to a VR headset and connected chair.

Not only did Audi give their fans a game, but they allowed each consumer to craft their own version and star as the lead player. The activation was able to add value to the brand through longer, more meaningful consumer interactions. As well, it added value for the consumer with an an educational and tactile brand experience.

SOUTHWEST AIRLINES: BIRTHDAY VIDEO

ADULTS LIKE BIRTHDAY PARTIES, TOO

To show their most loyal flyers a bit of appreciation, Southwest Airlines crafted a birthday video that allowed the customer to play along. In a personalized email, Southwest's video shows employees grabbing instruments, dancing and playing a special birthday song. The messaging included the name of the recipient and the conga-line style party had a personalized feel, delivered on their birthday.

The interactive part came in when the video prompted the birthday boy or girl to add their own sounds to the mix. For a minute, the frequent flyer could choose between drums, bells, horns and other instruments to craft their very own birthday tune which was then followed by a firework celebration and a message from the entire Rapid Rewards frequent flyer team.

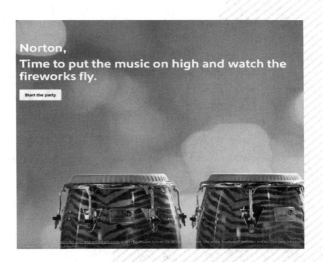

Norton,
Time to put the music on high and watch the fireworks fly.

Start the party

The playfulness of this should not be under-emphasized. Who would expect to see pilots playing bongos and flight attendants beating on steel drums? This effectively over delivers on the message, "we know you fly for business but some days you need to have fun."

CREDIT KARMA:
THE KARMA GAME

A GLIMPSE AT YOUR POTENTIAL FUTURE

Engaging millennials in a conversation about their financial future was the perfect fodder for a game. Taking off on the classic game, "MASH," which predicts if the player will live in a Mansion, Apartment, Shack or House, the KARMA game was launched.

Digital videos were produced in six second segments that determined how the player would end up with Kids, Auto, Realty, Marriage and Assets. The player loaded their headshot onto the game and started by spinning a wheel of magic numbers.

In the 15 seconds while that propagated, a 30 second video was randomly created. One of 27,000 combinations of the "potential" future was shown.

Users then pushed out the video to their friends or tried the game again. But either way, they spent a few moments thinking about their financial situation.

E&J BRANDY

SHAKING UP A ROUND WITH YOUR LONG LOST FRIENDS

In order to launch a new flavor variety, E&J leaned into friends of friends with an interactive game that encouraged consumers to make their own music video.

The game acknowledged Facebook protocols and randomly inserted friends into a custom shareable hip hop track that allowed consumers to get into the spirit of content creation.

The content itself sells the brand as a part of a defined lifestyle and the tone of the visuals feels the same as personalized content that friends share every day.

Authentic partners, Ebbets Field Flannels and Grado Headphones, created custom prizes that rewarded the best videos.

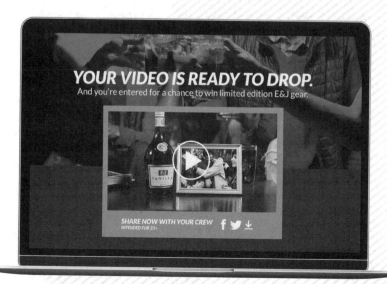

GOOD FOR THE SOUL

Much has been written on the overall concept of "Do Good," including Anne Bahr Thompson's inspiring book with the same title.

///

The higher purpose of "Brand Citizenship®" needs a budget and a mission for fulfillment.

Thompson explains that businesses need to look inward at their internal process and activities, as well as outward to what matters most to people.

Along the way, though, it still takes the right idea. That can take two forms:

• Developing original ideas that champion your brand's mantra.

• Joining an existing platform and enlisting its audience.

Both are compelling building blocks for communities. One objective may be the good PR or reputation management that evolves. Positive consumer responses can take the form of more usage, deeper relationships or shareable content.

CREATE A COMMON
LANGUAGE

CONSUMER
CO-CREATION

GAMIFY YOURSELF

GOOD FOR THE SOUL

FUEL THE
FLAME

IGNITE
THE FIRE

REI CO-OP: EVENTS

THINKING OUT OF THE STORE AND OUT OF THE BOX

REI makes two-way communication tangible with their Co-op events. Calling all of its regulars "shareholders," the retailer offers thousands of events each week in cities across the nation. The overall mission: connect with their consumers and share the love of the outdoors. The classes and outings range in topic from snow sports and climbing to wilderness medicine and stewardship.

Each class is led by REI personnel. Consumers not only walk away learning valuable outdoor skills but also with the opportunity to have had a direct conversation with the brand. For REI, this kind of access to consumers' thoughts and knowledge base is invaluable.

BACKPACKING
HOW TO CHOOSE BACKPACKING TENTS

For one, consumers become more knowledgeable about the brand and are encouraged to purchase REI products for their adventures. At the same time, the brand can highlight the fact that they are active in their local community and giving back by sharing knowledge and skills.

However, the most important part is that the brand gives the consumers valuable tactile practice. Armed with the competence to attack their next adventure and a deeply human brand experience, these consumers now go out into the world. They spread the word about REI and come back for more with their friends.

STELLA ARTOIS
AND WATER.ORG

1 LIMITED EDITON STELLA ARTOIS = 1 MONTH OF CLEAN WATER*

HELP END THE
GLOBAL WATER CRISIS

© 2018 AB InBev UK Limited. *For each pint, bottle and/or can sold, Stella Artois will donate £0.06 to water.org for the facts **drinkaware.co.uk**

PARTNERS IN BEER + WATER

Beer is over 90% water, so a decision to promote water, specifically clean drinking water, was a natural global platform for Stella Artois.

In 2015, a strategic partnership with Water.org was established and built upon annually. The campaign supports Water.org's mission to raise awareness and funds for the growing water crisis in developing countries.

Water.org and Stella Artois recognized that for those without clean water it took an exorbitant amount of time each day to gather water, time that should be spent pursuing dreams and enjoying life. So, they began spreading the message.

STELLA ARTOIS
Belgium

= **5** YEARS
CLEAN
WATER

MORE THAN 1 MILLION LIVES CHANGED

LEARN MORE BY VISITING:
water.org/stellaartois

To bring the consumer into the fold, the brand commissioned special editions of its signature pour glass. The partnership enlisted female artists in underserved nations to design "drinking chalices" inspired by their countries. For each glass purchased, a contribution of $3.13 is made, the equivalent of five years of clean drinking water for a single individual.

The partnership has been promoted with Matt Damon as an official spokesperson and has gained consumer awareness through content distributed on multiple channels. The overall plan is to provide water access to 3.5 million people by 2020.

SEVENLY

GOOD CAUSES ARE THEIR BUSINESS

Sevenly, one of the leading 'social good' companies operates on a belief that 'People Matter.' Working with selected nonprofits and artists, Sevenly designs a range of apparel and accessories themed around various global causes like LGBT rights, safe drinking water and children's education.

Each purchase gives back to the partnered nonprofit through monetary donations, actions and awareness. In just five years, Sevenly has been able to donate nearly $5 million through the sale of cause art as well as thousands of volunteer hours and products.

Wearing art that gives back inspires generosity but also acts as a walking billboard for Sevenly and the partnered nonprofit. By making cause marketing fashionable, Sevenly is able to give consumers something to talk about.

HÄAGEN-DAZS: HD LOVES HB

Häagen-Dazs loves Honey Bees

LET'S BEE SERIOUS ABOUT ICE CREAM

HD loves HB. In other words, Häagen-Dazs is all about the honey bees. During the height of the honey bee population crash, Häagen-Dazs launched a campaign to educate the public on the importance of the honey bees and provide support to research facilities.

Their year-long campaign consisted of a research grant to Penn State, a new honey flavored ice cream, partnerships with National Geographic and Martha Stewart Living, paper ads that were plantable due to embedded seeds, an emotional and educational public video and a "Bee Graffiti" contest on Facebook.

With 40% of their flavors dependent upon honey bees, Häagen-Dazs' campaign was not just a one-off to capture attention from a national crisis. By aligning with a meaningful cause that had a direct tie to their brand, Häagen-Dazs was able to come across as genuine without having to ask anything of consumers, other than enjoying their ice cream.

In just one week, the campaign generated 125 million PR impressions. By the end of the year, unaided brand awareness increased from 29% to 36%.

BURGER KING

CLOSE SHAVE FOR THE KING

Burger King has an open brief to keep its connections going with consumers in real time.

So it's no surprise that the marketing team made the connection to jump onto the Movember bandwagon with their own unique take on the charitable event.

The annual November campaign challenges "Mo-Bros" to grow moustaches to spread awareness of men's health issues. In a short video ad, Mr. Burger King himself visits a barber shop to have his iconic thick beard and moustache shaved off.

The freshly shaven King then challenged fans to grow an epic moustache and share their progress on social media with the hashtag #KingstacheChallenge. His stunt was complemented by a profile on Movember.com that collected $40,000 in donations for the foundation.

FUEL THE FLAME

OBJECTIVE
Unite believers to build your brand.

JOIN THE BRAND STRATEGY
Create opportunities for consumers to be involved in brand communication.

THOUGHT STARTERS
Think about:

• Getting people to rally around your message. How can you create a common language? (i.e. The Jeep Wave is a natural gesture that simply says, 'we get it', to everything Jeep stands for.)

• How can your product transcend the moment? (i.e. Essie names each polish based on inspirations and feelings that relate to how consumers want to feel when wearing it.)

• Where are opportunities to co-create? Can you provide personalization? Could consumer ideas launch a brand platform? (i.e. Xbox recognized consumers' passion for the game and let fans extend fandom to designing their own controllers.)

• When is the right moment to entertain your fans? (i.e. Chipotle's 'Cado Crusher not only educates, but rewards with coupons, driving people into the restaurant.)

• Supporting your people and what they care about creates feel good mentality all around. (i.e. Sevenly built their business model with the intention of serving various global causes.)

CHAPTER TEN

PASS THE TORCH

Once you build a fanbase, you can leverage existing fans by enlisting them. Being a part of your community can mean earning status, completing applications or offering limited spots and challenges.

With a solid base of identity and shareable content, the value of membership makes passing the torch a logical next step.

Supporting superfans and loyalists pays off with exponential brand endorsement. Once they've seen the value of being in the family, the opportunities to engage just keep coming.

Welcome to your extended family.

INFLUENCER NETWORK

It's your club. So you can write the rules. With an established brand value that exceeds product function, you're ready for style points.

//

Membership can include special perks that enhance your value proposition and allow you to require certain activities or attributes in selecting your members.

Most importantly, it's your opportunity to set the language, tone and personality of your branded community. You can be serious, quirky, informative, useful or helpful as long as you stay true to who you are.

PASS THE TORCH

INFLUENCER NETWORK

CONSUMER IS THE COMMUNICATION

CONTROL THE BUZZ

FAMILY TIES

FUEL THE FLAME

IGNITE THE FIRE

THE SKIMM

WHAT ARE SKIMMBASSADORS?

People who Skimm and love it and want to get more involved. The Skimm'bassador program is a way for Skimm'rs to connect with us at SkimmHQ, while helping with different grassroots marketing initiatives and product testing. They represent theSkimm in their cities & communities and help us grow through word of mouth. They brainstorm with our team on new ideas, give feedback, and get some sneak peeks along the way. They become our interns and partners. Oh, and they get Skimm swag.

theSkimm

NO ADS, JUST REWARDS FOR FRIENDS

The concept behind theSkimm is almost as good as the daily condensed news email itself. It's a fun, easy, entertaining read but at its heart it's a business model based upon friends of friends.

Everyone can become a Skimm'bassador, they just need to recruit ten friends to sign up. This makes them a part of the club, where they'll be entitled to get a few freebies along the way.

Where do the freebies come from? Therein lies the rub. It's what sponsors are willing to pay to be included in the conversation. Anything from vacations to cosmetics and everything in between.

Signing up as a Skimm'bassador is much like any other ambassador program where new leads are traded for swag and exclusive event invites.

Each branded piece of swag comes with a "price tag" of a certain number of referrals. The wine sippy cup is one of the most coveted pieces of merch but also the hardest to obtain at 200 subscribers. By giving their ambassadors a clear reward system, theSkimm is able to put the power in the hands of their fans and let them work as hard as they want.

However, theSkimm's effectiveness is not only a result of their branded gear. Skimm'bassadors are given the first chance at opportunities like internships, jobs, scholarships, product testing and input on marketing campaigns. They also meet at skimmHQ and with other Skimm'bassadors to plan city-wide events, like Sip 'n Skimm.

By creating a partnership with their ambassadors, rather than an army, they are empowering their fans to spread brand awareness and activate their social networks.

Currently, there are over 12,000 Skimm'bassadors both in and out of college and 5+ million Skimm readers everyday. The Skimm partners raised $15+ million from venture capitalists as well as encouraging 120,000 people to vote in the 2016 election.

SEPHORA BEAUTY INSIDER

New!

Beauty INSIDER
COMMUNITY

EXPLORE NOW ▸

CREATE A PROFILE ▸

EVERY BEAUTY TALKS
Get honest answers from real people.

JOIN THE CONVERSATION ▸

IN GOOD COMPANY
Discover beauty content tailored to your interests.

FIND GROUPS ▸

BEAUTY LOOKS
Browse inspiration for your summer look.

CHECK OUT THE GALLERY ▸

JUMP INTO THE POOL WITH YOUR NEW BFFS

The Beauty Insider Community is a pool platform where everyone who has a passion for makeup can chat about beauty or other interests. They interact by:

• Posting photos

• Joining groups

• Recommending products

• Chatting live with other shoppers

• Giving and sharing advice

• Checking on upcoming events

By becoming a Beauty Insider, consumers are rewarded points every time they shop. Information and inclusion are strategically aligned with two-way conversations and the ability to submit a profile and introduce oneself to the group. With a little help from their friends, users can view the online gallery of photos and tag the product to help others create similar looks.

The Beauty Insider Community not only gives loyal fans a place to interact with each other, but it builds credibility for Sephora products in perpetuity. Ultimately, the brand is a bystander, out of the way, yet helping its fans become experts on all things beauty, including their products.

SOUTHERN TIDE: AMBASSADOR PROGRAM

MARKETING WITH COLLEGE MARKETERS

Southern Tide has followed the successful model of many other lifestyle brands by employing their own fleet of ambassadors. The ambassadors, who are mainly comprised of college students, hold on-campus events, giveaway swag and regularly post photos and news about the brand on their social media.

The strategy focuses a little more closely on each individual and the competition to "Wear the Tide" is a tough evaluation. There's an element of the brand's bravado that needs to come through, so it's not a paint by numbers, me-too, college program.

The brand does a good job of using dynamic personalities to leverage their own social networks within Greek life organizations, college clubs, sports teams and extracurricular activities.

Although brand information and programming are important, the brand lets ambassadors focus on the Southern Tide culture and forming deeper emotional connections.

SOUTHERN TIDE
AMBASSADORS
PROGRAM

SOUTHERN TIDE

COLLEGE AMBASSADORS

ZACK FLANAGAN
UNIVERSITY OF LOUISVILLE
@zack_flanagan

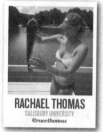

RACHAEL THOMAS
SALISBURY UNIVERSITY
@raeethomas

COOPER ALLISON
KANSAS STATE UNIVERSITY
@cooperkay

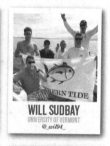

WILL SUDBAY
UNIVERSITY OF VERMONT
*@_wil94_*

MEGAN LUCAS
UNIVERSITY OF HAWAII
@meg_luc

TJ CHRISTINO
JAMES MADISON UNIVERSITY
@tjchristino

SARAH QUERY
AUBURN UNIVERSITY
@sarahquery

IAN PETERSON
UNIVERSITY OF NORTH DAKOTA
@ianpeterson23

CHOLULA HOT SAUCE: THE ORDER OF CHOLULA

BOSS OF THE SAUCE CELEBRATES REAL FANS

Cholula Hot Sauce recognized the impact their brand had on many of their consumers' lives, from getting the bottle tattooed on their body to bringing their personal supply into every restaurant.

In response, they created "The Order of Cholula," an online community dedicated to their most loyal superfans. They enlisted a handful of top influencers including artists, musicians and athletes:

• MLB pitcher Noah Syndergaard

• YouTube star Brian Poirer

• MMA Fighter Scott Holtzman

The brand calls them "Cholulians," and made them members of the original chapter. These Cholulians then shared their stories through a series of short films and encouraged their fanbases to join one of the five flavor-based chapters.

The first 1,000 fans to sign up were given a bottle of the limited-edition small-batch Sweet Habanero as well as access to content, longer forms of the original films, discounts and merchandise.

While the brand likes to claim that membership is selective and reserved for only the most dedicated, any level of fan can earn their membership card after filling out a form documenting their first experience with the hot sauce.

From there, superfans can choose to fill out an entire profile complete with a photo and story for a chance to be featured as the Cholulian of the month. The community also encourages members to upload their artwork, whether it be a painting of the bottle or a custom jeans-bottle holder, so that other Cholulians can find inspiration in one another.

CONSUMER IS THE COMMUNICATION

As your brand expression becomes real and consumers are willing to talk about you, it's time to give them the opportunity to make your brand their own.

///

Consumers have seen enough actors saying they care about a brand or a belief. There is nothing genuine in those one-way messages.

However, where there is belief, there can be more and no one believes in your brand more than your superfans. At some point, they may not only say it better, they may become the ideator and communicator.

PASS THE TORCH

INFLUENCER NETWORK

CONSUMER IS THE COMMUNICATION

CONTROL THE BUZZ

FAMILY TIES

FUEL THE FLAME

IGNITE THE FIRE

REI: #OPTOUTSIDE

THE DECLARATION OF OUTDOOR INDEPENDENCE

REI made a bold move in 2015 when it decided to shut its doors on the biggest shopping day of the year, Black Friday. Instead of asking consumers to race through its aisles at the crack of dawn, it asked them to go outside and spend the day with family and friends, enjoying the company of nature.

They paid their 12,000 employees, closed all 143 retail locations, both distribution centers and their headquarters in what quickly became known as the "#optoutside" movement.

#optoutside

The movement has quickly grown to include partnerships with major brands like Lyft (who offered $10 off rides to public parks and lands) and Subaru (who helped bring shelter dogs to the outdoors), involvement from 170 nonprofits and organizations and pledges from 1.4 million people.

A cornerstone of the #optoutside campaign has been the amount of user-generated content shared and promoted on social channels. REI has made consumers proud to opt outside and as a result there have been over 7.5 million posts on Instagram with the hashtag.

The movement has its heart in the brand's values. Operating as a co-op, REI believes that "time in the outdoors makes us healthier and happier." This is a mission that their members and fans feel strongly about, too. Therefore, by using the content from consumers they are able to share this combined passion and spread it in a way that is extremely authentic and persuading.

SEPHORA

NOW FEATURING YOUR BEAUTY CONSULTANTS

As the definition and standards in beauty are ever-changing, advertising in the beauty world has the oppurtunity to broaden their message. To tackle expectations from consumers, beauty brand Sephora wanted to make sure that the message they communicated was one of diversity, inclusion and passion. Instead of casting models, they looked internally.

Who better to represent their brand than their own employees, who also happen to be very dedicated Sephora customers? With over 11,000 employees in their North American stores, Sephora had plenty of faces and stories to share. Ultimately the brand chose 10 of its cast members out of 1,000 who submitted entries.

The campaign, was titled "Reach Out and Gift."

- It suggested beauty products to give during the holiday season.
- It helped address the challenge of buying makeup for others.
- It featured the added excitement of showing the people who can help you do it.

Sephora recognized that beauty can be hard to gift because it is deeply personal and many consumers are unaware of the array of products available for different lifestyles and skin types. By using their own extremely diverse employees, they hoped to spark ideas about gifts and show that beauty means something different to everyone.

Their campaign featured a Moroccan color consultant with a hijab, a product consultant with alopecia, a young man who works as a senior skincare advisor and an artist from Missouri whose beauty style is a mix between girly and rock 'n' roll. While the ads were placed nationwide, the hometowns of these models received special window unveilings.

//

REI: FORCE OF NATURE

TRUE STORIES OF EVEN TRUER WOMEN

REI realized that when outdoor sports are portrayed, a significant percentage features males. The imagery, call to actions and stories were heavily one sided and they decided to change that.

To start, they conducted a national study that proved what they had thought. Sixty-three percent of women could not identify a female outdoor role model and a majority felt that a man's interest in the outdoors was given more attention than a woman's. To combat this issue, they launched "Force of Nature" a campaign designed to disrupt the status quo.

REI invested $1 million for community programs dedicated to women in the outdoors, partnered with other brands to redesign gear for women and offered more than 1,000 co-op events targeted at women.

Supporting the campaign:

• A partnership with Outside magazine and the first "all women's issue."

• A film festival with movies that feature women in the outdoors.

• A digital hub filled with two-way connectivity, stories, trips, events and gear.

Within eight months there were 250,000 photos posted on Instagram with #forceofnature.

NYX MAKEUP

CONTENT BY CONSUMERS FOR CONSUMERS

NYX is the pied piper of makeup. Their execution strategy? Send consumers products to try and they will return the favor with user-generated content (UGC).

The brand moved completely away from showing models for its products and features only real consumers who use their brand and send in photos and commentary.

The consumer created content that finds its way onto NYX's social feeds is accompanied by detailed captions explaining application techniques, preferences and tips.

What started as a leap of faith turned into a movement, highlighting influencers in mass. Nearly every image on NYX's social feeds and website features an unedited photo from one of their consumers.

Here's what they found:

• Shoppers engage with seven UGC photos per visit.

• Interactions from UGC convert at 320% higher rate.

• Average order volume is 93% higher with UGC content.

As a result, NYX's fanbase has grown exponentially. Year-over-year social engagement rose 97%, ranking third in highest engagement for cosmetics companies and follower size has reached over 12 million on Instagram alone.

CURATORS OF SWEDEN

NOMINATE   ABOUT   CURRENT CURATOR   ARCHIVE   Follow

JENNY THEOLIN

was @sweden   2015-03-02 to 2015-03-09

THE PEOPLE HAVE TWEETED

The country of Sweden has decided to make its Twitter account completely run by its own citizens. This was a bold move that spoke more about who the country really is than any single community manager ever could.

The campaign, titled "Curators of Sweden," aims to show the world a diverse and inclusive view of what it means to be a part of their nation. Each week a different Swede is given access to the account where they are encouraged to share their interests, thoughts on national news and showcase their personal stories.

The end result? A view of Sweden that is unlike anything a typical media outlet can convey. Since each individual has their own point-of-view, it makes the country more interesting and ultimately more human. A perfect way to break the ice.

350+ people have had their voices heard since the start of Curators of Sweden in 2011.

Sweden
Sverige
CURATORS OF SWEDEN

I'M @sweden / Hasan
@sweden
A new Swede every week! / Your crooked guide to the Swedish suburbian safari.
Sweden http://www.curatorsofsweden.com

I'M @sweden / Sonja
@sweden
A new Swede every week / Holy mother of two. Grew up side by side with awesome nature. 27 years old. This is exciting.
Sweden http://www.curatorsofsweden.com

HONDA: #HONDANEXTDOOR

COVET THY NEIGHBOR'S CR-V

Honda realized that fans make the best salespeople. Because they don't have many dealerships in France, they decided to create car salesmen out of current Honda drivers.

#HondaNextDoor was a three-week long campaign throughout France that turned real Honda owners' garages into mini dealerships. Honda worked with brand superfans to convert their garages into suitable places for the public.

Honda teams installed logos above garages and added a few flags but they let the fans keep all of their knick-knacks and collectables. After all, the branded toy cars, posters and memorabilia that already filled the shelves of these garages told a compelling story.

Since the mission was to promote the sale of their CR-V and HR-V models they invited customers to visit the mini dealerships and test drive their neighbor's car. They then let their fans do the rest of the work. Potential owners were able to ask questions and receive candid answers from a trusted source.

Thousands of potential leads were gathered, over one million people were reached, and at least 1,000 drivers signed up for a test run. Honda is now rolling out the campaign throughout the rest of Europe.

J.CREW: #CASTMEJCREW

A HAPPY HOLIDAY STORY

In order to enhance its place at the holiday table, J.Crew came up with a message encouraging its fans to be a part of the brand.

"How do you J.Crew?" was the question J.Crew asked its fans in their latest UGC centered campaign. During the 2017 holiday season, J.Crew lovers were encouraged to upload their photos showing how they make J.Crew part of their holiday.

Any photo on Instagram or Twitter with the hashtag #castmejcrew was entered into a contest held by the brand. The winners would be chosen by the retailer and given the opportunity to be cast in a future J.Crew photo shoot.

At last count, there were more than 7,000 photos on Instagram with the hashtag.

#castmejcrew

CONTROL THE BUZZ

You're at the party. You've brought good ideas to consumers. They're interacting with you.

///

Your brand is in the conversation.

Good vibes are happening.

The more there is, the more popular you'll be.

A little suggestive selling is now in order.

PASS THE TORCH

INFLUENCER NETWORK

CONSUMER IS THE COMMUNICATION

CONTROL THE BUZZ

FAMILY TIES

FUEL THE FLAME

IGNITE THE FIRE

KENTUCKY FRIED CHICKEN

THAT COLONEL IS SUCH A JOKER

KFC has been inserting themselves in the conversation for the last several years with the revolving Colonels and a spunky personality.

The idea is that no consumer wants to work hard to think about their next meal and fun, affordable food fits the bill. They've brought that tone to their entire marketing mix and are used to having fun with consumers.

So they gamed the system and thought it would be interesting to see how long it took fans to figure out that their Twitter account was promoting the brand's famous seasoning of 11 herbs and spices.

Here was the hidden joke: @KFC only follows 11 people—five women and six men on Twitter. This observation wasn't enough to stir up the social media world until one user pointed out that the 11 followers were:

Five former Spice Girls + Six guys name Herb = 11 HERBS AND SPICES

A single user found it and it went viral. The commotion gathered so much attention that people started investigating the original tweeter and making claims that the whole thing was a setup. Of course, he denied he had any connection or prior knowledge about the account, but the conversation soon turned towards his background and away from KFC.

Edge
@edgette22
Follow

.@KFC follows 11 people.

Those 11 people? 5 Spice Girls and 6 guys named Herb.

11 Herbs & Spices. I need time to process this.

12:59 PM - 19 Oct 2017

323,170 Retweets 716,076 Likes

4.7K 323K 716K

In response, KFC sent the user a hand-painted portrait of himself riding piggyback style on KFC's own Colonel Sanders. The painting was outrageous. Aside from the fan holding a KFC drumstick while propped on the back of the prestigious founder, it features a majestic mountain scene complete with a sunset, wild forest animals and a Loch Ness monster.

The act was so over-the-top that it worked. In less than 24 hours thousands of people had commented on and retweeted the painting post, effectively shifting the conversation back to KFC and it's creativity.

IKEA: FRAKTA BAG

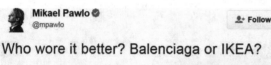

Mikael Pawlo ✓
@mpawlo

2+ Follow

Who wore it better? Balenciaga or IKEA?

FASHION CAN BE TIMELY

When fashion house Balenciaga released their "Area Extra Large Shopper" bag in early 2017, the internet went crazy. It wasn't the $2,145 price tag that astonished consumers the most; it was the bag's uncanny resemblance to IKEA's iconic "Frakta" bag.

The blue carry all from the Swedish brand Ikea set buyers back $0.99 and wasn't considered a fashion accessory until the exact moment Balenciaga released theirs.

Immediately social media lit up. Twitter users joked about finally being able to afford a piece of high fashion and how to help one another make sure they accidently don't buy the wrong bag.

Not only did this release stir up the social media world, but it sparked creativity in the DIY world. Inspired by Balenciaga, brand fans soon turned their own Frakta bags into works of fashion ranging from undergarments, to shoes, to cell phone purses.

IKEA's response to all of this? An ad.

The ad showed an image of their product below the simple statement, "How to identify an original IKEA FRAKTA bag."

How to identify an original
IKEA FRAKTA bag.

MULTIFUNCTIONAL
It can carry hockey gear,
bricks and even water.

SHAKE IT
If it rustles, it's
the real deal.

PRICE TAG
Only $0.99

FOLD IT
Are you able to fold it to the
size of a small purse? If the answer
is yes, congratulations.

THROW IT IN THE DIRT
If you feel comfortable getting
your bag dirty, knowing you
can easily rinse it off, it's real.

The ad was a humorous guide pointing out fail-safe methods to 'ensure' consumers were using an authentic IKEA bag:

• One of those methods suggested throwing the bag in the dirt. "A true FRAKTA is simply rinsed off with a garden hose when dirty."

• Perhaps the best line was: "PRICE TAG: only $0.99."

Their straightforward yet sarcastic ad pushed back at Balenciaga and reopened the floodgates on social media. It gave fans something new to talk about and directed their conversation back to some of the brand's core values:

• Being humble

• Unique

• Cost-conscious

By playing into the buzz instead of trying to silence it, IKEA was able to shine the spotlight on themselves while keeping an authentic tone that their fans expect.

SOUTHWEST

HEY FRIEND, IT'S YOUR AIRLINE

Employees that work in all sectors of Southwest go through extensive training to learn the tone, style and voice of the brand.

By using UGC and sharing experiences, the brand is able to respond in real time to consumer's concerns, questions and comments as well as react to happy consumers with their well-known GIFs.

They also strategically turn common complaints and frustrations into stories highlighting the brand and its employees. The concept of using GIFs of employees waving, saluting or winking instead of verbal response is sometimes all that it takes to reinforce the relationship.

Although rare, situations do happen and it takes a proactive approach to keep the conversation positive. Southwest's policy of publicly thanking their hardworking employees and sharing stories as they happen in real time brings everyone together.

//

NETFLIX: LUKE'S DINER

COFFEE + FANS + PHOTOS = MORE BUZZ

The release of a *Gilmore Girls* epilogue had fans of the original series turning to social media to share their excitement.

Trailers on YouTube were registering millions of views and thousands of comments and hashtags like #GilmoreGirlsRevival were being used tens of thousands of times across social media.

Netflix, being the exclusive viewing platform for the new follow-up, bought into this buzz by transforming over 200 cafes into set replicas.

Luke's Diner was a fictional cafe in the show where many of the most memorable scenes took place. To tap into fans' love and connection for the diner, Netflix outfitted cafes across the country to look just like Luke's and served free coffee to the first 250 fans.

For one day only, superfans were able to stop by the pop-up diners and immerse themselves in the fictional world of *Gilmore Girls.* Of course, Netflix used the spot to promote its brand by hiding secret codes for free Netflix subscriptions in the sleeves of coffee cups.

The stunt resulted in lines hundreds deep outside each cafe and thousands of social media posts. Data released from Snapchat gives a look at just how successful the campaign was. A Netflix branded Snapchat filter was accessed via a QR code printed on 10,000 coffee cups. The filter was viewed 880,000 times, reaching over 500,000 people in just one day.

CRAFTSMAN CLUB

KNOW-HOW TAKES KNOW-HOW

Certainly, the grandparent of all brand communities is the Craftsman Club. Created in 1993 to serve its most loyal fans, the Craftsman Club provided a platform to share their skills and enthusiasm for a line of products built specifically for makers.

There were great reasons to join:

• Trusted products

• Powerful brand

• Exclusivity for members

The screeching sound and slow connectivity of the internet in 1993 did not stop the momentum of superfans who were proud to call themselves craftsmen. In its 25 years since launching, the Craftsman Club has welcomed over 15 million members and has changed owners from Sears to Stanley Black and Decker.

The current site features:

• An inspiration board (curated) to spark interest

• A projects section for community discussion

• Members only events/challenges

WENDY'S

YO WENDY'S, HOW ABOUT ENGAGING WITH ME?

Carter Wilkerson made Twitter history when he tweeted at Wendy's asking how many retweets he needed for a year of free chicken nuggets.

Wendy's prompt reply of "18 million" set off a storm of tweets supporting Carter and sharing his message. With over 3.6 million retweets, Carter became one of the most retweeted users in Twitter history.

Wendy's recognized his accomplishment (although it was well short of 18 million) with a year of free nugs and a $100k donation to the Dave Thomas Foundation for Adoption.

Wilkerson spent 15 minutes in the spotlight earning more attention from Wendy's, Ellen DeGeneres, Twitter and other celebrities.

Carter now hosts his own website, nuggsforcarter.com and sells t-shirts. All proceeds from the t-shirt sales are donated to the Dave Thomas Foundation for Adoption.

CHACOS

GO WHERE YOUR FEET TAKE YOU

What came first, ChacoNation or the signature tan? At its heart are dedicated fans who love the shoes and badge their unique toe tans in photos. The "Chaco's tan" has become a symbol of pride amongst the outdoorsy, and Chacos has fully embraced it.

The brand created a community called ChacoNation, to share news, stories, events and invite fans to share photos of their shoes (and tan lines) using the hashtag #ChacoNation, which currently has over 54,000 posts on Instagram.

They helped build this community by hosting Chaco tan line competitions in 2010, 2011, 2012 and 2016. The contest asked fans to submit their best Chaco tan and the person whose photo received the most likes, wins. The interesting thing is, other outdoorsy brands have also adapted Chacos tan-line competitions, like Rock Creek, Kinnucan's, Blue Ridge Outdoors and BackCountry. There is currently no information released on the results of these contests.

Ultimately, Chaco consumers share a passion for the product and the adventurous lifestyle the brand represents. By listening to their fans and giving them an outlet to share their pride, Chaco was able to take a consumer craze and turn it into an ownable brand element.

FAMILY TIES

Once they love you, it's time for the next step.

///

Inviting fans to your house, i.e. including them in anything about your brand that makes them feel like it's their house, will enhance the warm feelings.

Brands have found that even the most basic parts of their story have resonated deeply with fans.

Some fans go so far as not only branding themselves, but branding their lifestyles.

PASS THE TORCH

INFLUENCER NETWORK

CONSUMER IS THE COMMUNICATION

CONTROL THE BUZZ

FAMILY TIES

FUEL THE FLAME

IGNITE THE FIRE

STARBURSTS DRESS

Hi Emily,
We hope you enjoy this stash of Starburst! Looking forward to your next unexplainably silly design.

-Your friends
at Starburst

WEAR IT + SHARE IT

Everyone has their favorite candy and most people eat more of it than they would probably like to admit.

For most, the candy is just a supplement to snack time or a reward for a tough workout. But for Emily Seilhamer, candy plays a much bigger role in her life. Starbursts are a regular part of her diet and her relationship.

Emily met her future husband in college when he offered her a Starburst. As their relationship grew so did the number of wrappers of their favorite candy. Soon, Emily had hundreds of wrappers in many colors and felt inspired to "upcycle" them into a work of art.

That art turned out to be a dress made of more than 10,000 wrappers. Following the creation of the dress, Emily's then-boyfriend proposed which meant the dress had to make a special appearance at the wedding.

As expected, Starbursts took notice of Emily's creation and devotion to their brand, and sent her a large personalized candy jar to keep the creations going.

Even though the dress is complete, Emily has continued to upcycle the wrappers into wearables like purses and has plans for future projects as well.

TARGET WEDDING

MATRIMONY IN AISLE NINE

Monthly Target visits are a staple errand in many households around the U.S. But, for Target superfans Michael Delvalle and Isabella Sablan, "regular visits" meant visiting the chain up to three times a week.

The couple found that browsing the aisles and shopping for clearance items or finding something to bake kept them from a boring weeknight at home.

Eventually, when they decided to get married, they knew Target had to play a role in their big day. Unable to host their reception at the store, they opted for fun and down-to-earth photos that showcased some of the realities of marriage.

The couple's photos show how much brands can play into our everyday lives. Seemingly small life events like picking out house décor or gathering ingredients can turn into bigger memories when a brand begins to add value and establish a relationship with the consumer.

In the case of Michael and Isabella, the brand entered their inner circle by winning their trust, providing solutions for everyday needs and entertaining them on slow evenings.

In doing this, Target gained enthusiastic brand advocates that will continue to spread the brand's message.

TACO BELL

NOW SERVING SPICY VEGAS WEDDINGS

To celebrate the opening of the chapel in their flagship store, Taco Bell held a "Love and Tacos" contest to find the first couple to be married Taco Bell style. Over 150 couples submitted entries and 17,000 people voted on their stories.

In the end, one couple won the ultimate Las Vegas Taco Bell wedding experience. Aside from branded merchandise and professional wedding services, the lucky couple won airfare for six, entry to a spa, accommodations, VIP table status at a club and tickets to amusement rides.

Taco Bell later opened their chapel doors to the public so that all superfans could experience a branded wedding. A wedding at the flagship currently costs $600 and takes 30 minutes.

The wedding package includes an ordained officiant, a reception area, catering in the form of a Taco 12 Pack and Cinnabon cake, branded merchandise like "just married" tees, a sauce packet garter, as well as a sauce packet bouquet.

TACO BELL SENIOR PICS

MOST LIKELY TO CRUNCH A GORDITA

Weddings aren't the only big life memory being created at Taco Bell. Seniors graduating high school and college have been flocking to the chain to use it as the backdrop for their senior pictures.

It started when a St. Louis area high schooler joked on Twitter about taking her senior pictures at the fast food joint. After the tweet garnered attention from her peers, she followed through with her promise and posted the final images to social media. Buzz took off and soon she was being interviewed on TV and featured on Taco Bell's website.

For the other seniors who have followed in her footsteps, the pictures are an inside joke among friends or an attempt to be recognized by the brand. For many, their attempt paid off.

A page on Taco Bell's website promises to feature anyone who posts their photos with the hashtag #TacoBellSenior. So far 12 seniors have been featured with dozens more on Twitter and Instagram hoping to earn a spot.

Taco Bell recognized that posing in a flower field is overrated and that your letterman jacket isn't anything special and saw a brand opportunity. By embracing their fans' enthusiasm with recognition, Taco Bell was able to help these seniors create lifelong memories and earn a place in their fans' lives.

CONVENIENTLY WED

FOUNTAINS OF JOY

Wawa might not be in our Top 100 list but apparently it tops the list for convenience store wedding locations. Multiple couples along the east coast have made Wawa the backdrop to their proposals, marriage ceremonies and wedding photos.

Not to be out done, fellow convenience store Circle K has also seen its share of newlyweds. For one new bride, the chain was a daily coffee stop on her morning commute. Then, when it came time to tie the knot, Circle K was there for her once again by providing a backdrop for some of her favorite wedding photos.

Integrating a brand into something as personal as a wedding not only showcases a superfan's love, but it brings the community together. For many, places like Wawa and Circle K are regular stops on the way to work and on weekend errands.

With frequent trips to the chain, employees and customers get to know one another and when major life events happen in store, it deepens that relationship while solidifying brand loyalty.

PASS THE TORCH

OBJECTIVE
Enlist fans to share your brand.

JOIN THE BRAND STRATEGY
Provide opportunities for consumers to take ownership of your brand through organic behavior, challenges and/or applications.

THOUGHT STARTERS
Think about:

• Why consumers want to be an ambassador for your brand. How can you support this behavior? What can you do to help them, help you? (i.e. Southern Tide consumers love wearing the brand and living the lifestyle. The brand solidified this behavior by providing swag and ambassador titles in exchange for ongoing brand conversation and promotion.)

• What consumers have already done with your brand. How can you leverage their behavior? How can you thank them? (i.e. Chaco recognized consumers take pride in their Chaco tan lines, thus starting the #ChacoNation community to celebrate the lines as the symbol of a true adventurer.)

• Recognizing fandom in your brand. What are superfans saying about your brand? In what ways do fans want your brand to be in their life? (i.e. One couple recognized the reality of married life would be enjoying the small things like shopping at Target. Not only did they register at Target, but took engagement photos there as well.)

CHAPTER ELEVEN

OWN, DON'T RENT

If we want consumers to come to us, we need to go to them.

We've illustrated the importance of brands understanding the connection their consumers have through community. We have also revealed the opportunities for brands when consumers become loyal fans who seek out content and share the brand's message.

But, many brands mistake followers for fandom and quantity of content for quality of relationship. Let's take a moment to look at how your brand can ensure you have the right people seeing the right message.

THE DISTRIBUTION THEORY

Find your hub

//

In the book, *The Content Trap*, Harvard professor Bharat Anand lays out the Theory of Distribution, which compares two different strategies for distributing content. In the example on page 287, Anand uses two media publishers, Huffington Post and The Bleacher Report, to showcase his theory. Let's take a look.

In both cases, the publisher acts as a hub for content, the difference comes with how each manages their content and where they drive their audience.

In the top diagram, Huffington Post is the starting point, the homebase for all its content. People sought out information starting there, but then were sent to various media channels.

Conversely, The Bleacher Report places shareable content across media channels first, all of which drive readers back to their owned hub or site. The difference between the two is the initial consumer interception, as well as where the consumer ends up.

DISTRIBUTION THEORY

The Content Trap: How Huffington Post and
Bleacher Report built audiences.

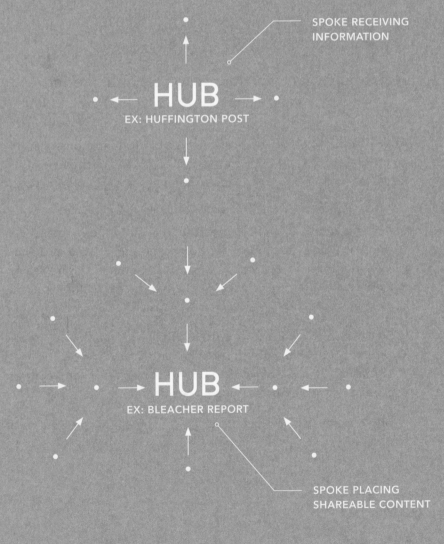

SPOKE RECEIVING
INFORMATION

HUB
EX: HUFFINGTON POST

HUB
EX: BLEACHER REPORT

SPOKE PLACING
SHAREABLE CONTENT

MINIMALIST THINKING STARTS HERE

Now apply that same theory to brand marketing.

//

As you begin to think about attracting the right consumers and creating a fanbase, think about it in the way The Bleacher Report does, by going to the audience instead of expecting them to come to you first.

We've showed how one-way messaging is no longer successful. While that type of top-down method of expecting your audience to see your message may have worked in the days of Pat Weaver, it simply no longer works because it does not reflect how people consume media today.

In an interview with Harvard Business Review, Anand explained, "Content is not simply about broadcasting information or news to your readers, it's also about facilitating conversation and connecting your readers. It creates all sorts of possibilities."

In other words, brands have to drive consumers back to a central hub in order to reinforce connection.

Driving consumers back to a central hub is the heart of communities. But how to center it?

This is where brands begin to veer off course.

We see many brand marketers wanting to pay publishers and influencers to instigate a connection.

They use these channels as the spokes from The Distribution Theory. The hope here is that endorsement becomes engagement.

This method has a role in gaining awareness, but can't be expected to create a brand community.

Ultimately, building your own audience with an authentic, single message is the optimal strategy.

RENT TO OWN, BUT DON'T RENT FOREVER.

We believe in the power of influence. Whether that be word of mouth, reviews, ads, links or videos—we know word of mouth is 2.5x more influential than advertisements.

//

Patrick Hanlon's 2016 TEDx Talk on Primal Branding explains the importance of your consumers' conversation: "It doesn't matter what you tell people about your product or service, it matters what they say about it. Eighty percent of people don't believe what you say in advertising and marketing materials anyway, so good luck finding the other 20%."

The question then becomes, who are you asking to provide influence and start conversation about your brand? If the answer is a medium that your brand doesn't own, then essentially you are renting your influence.

Let's take another look at the example from the previous page. A brand that pays an influential individual to post content on their Instagram page may be a great way to gain brand awareness, but the audience you are talking to is a rented crowd. They are fans of the influencer, not your brand.

Yet.

We believe the rent vs. own conversation regarding influencers depends on the state of your brand, product and category.

However, we also believe that if you choose to rent for awhile, the best bet is to focus on a single message to build the audience that you are renting. Eventually, your goal should be to stop renting and create loyalists of your own among the group.

The chart below gives you a good starting point to analyze where your brand lies today on the rent vs. own and inauthentic vs. authentic spectrums. Your goal is always the same. Create connections through renting but know that you must own your fanbase eventually.

Getting your brand to the "goal" means owning the content and conversation instead of borrowing and it allows you to build your brand hub.

THE GOAL

AUTHENTIC OWNERSHIP

FIVE STEPS TO BEING AN OWNER VS A RENTER:

01

BUILD YOUR AUDIENCE ON PLATFORMS YOU OWN.

Digital platforms will continue to change daily. Building your audience solely on social channels will not completely optimize your brand. Having followers is great, but it is challenging to consistently grow exponentially without an ownable strategy.

02

YOUR BUSINESS PLAN HAS TO INCLUDE BUILDING A COMMUNITY.

Since social platforms are pay to play, the KPI of your overall business strategy has to be building a loyal group of followers and creating a brand community.

03

BUILD YOUR EMAIL DATABASE.

Consider that loyalty can only be measured by fans who have exchanged data though email, ecommerce and personal connectivity. Building a database of email is the safest way to ensure your investment pays off.

04

BUILD PROGRAMMING AROUND YOUR BRAND THAT MOST CLOSELY ASSOCIATES WITH CONSUMER INTERESTS.

These programs change every few years, but don't change your message every time you execute a new plan. Stand for something and stick with it.

05

DON'T BUY SUPERFANS. YOU CAN EARN THEM.

Buying influencers is a variation of one-way messaging.
Paid influencers rarely create enough value to pay you back.

THE MARKETING MIND (IS KIND OF MADE UP)

As we completed our research and the preparation for this book, we fielded one more study.

//

Among other questions, we asked 100 C-level marketers how their brands are faring when it comes to engagement.

- 71% said the level of consumer engagement with their brand is either strong or very strong.

- 54% said their brand has a specific purpose that makes a tangible difference in daily lives.

- 48% said they somewhat invest in cultivating a community.

- 27% said their consumers interact with each other (online or in-person) regularly.

Overall, we found that community engagement is in the eye of the beholder. They did agree on the need to drive emotion. Emotion can help build belonging, connection, influence and ultimately lead to rewards and proud membership.

If your brand cultivates community, which of the following characteristics define it?

EMOTIONS — 58%

BELONGING — 46%

CONNECTION — 39%

INFLUENCE — 30%

REWARDS — 22%

MEMBERSHIP — 19%

Source: Moosylvania CMO Study with Shopper Stories, 2018

IF YOU'VE READ THIS FAR,

you know the power of building communities.

//

So, the next time your brand considers spending significantly on one-way tactics, here are a few questions you can ask:

• What would happen if we applied the same amount of spend on a two-way campaign? If the answer is that the reach can't be achieved, they're not innovating or problem solving. They're painting by numbers.

• How do you know the target consumer will actually spend their eight second attention span listening or watching this message? If they use the words "digital extension," tell them to start over.

• Why is the medium with the least amount of consumer engagement getting the greatest share of the budget? If they tell you they are hoping to make people buy the brand, ask what would happen if they joined the brand.

THANKS FOR SPENDING THE TIME WITH US.

To stay up to date with our latest research and see thousands more case studies visit nortycohen.com

Start here to uncover where you are in crafting your community

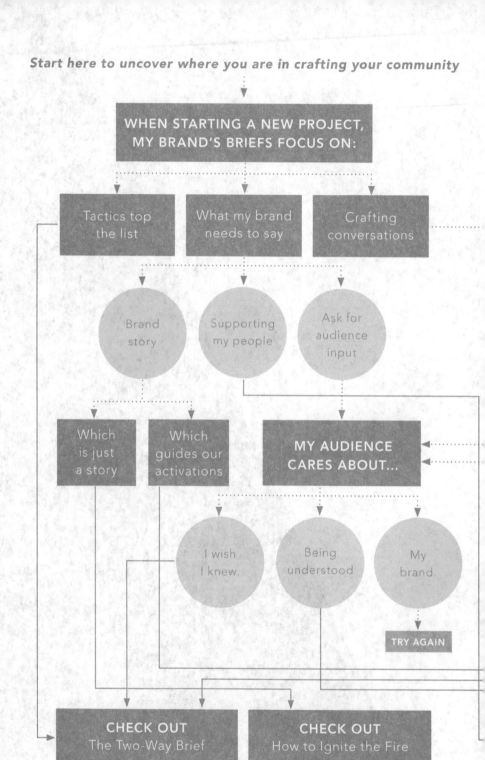

WHEN STARTING A NEW PROJECT, MY BRAND'S BRIEFS FOCUS ON:

Tactics top the list

What my brand needs to say

Crafting conversations

Brand story

Supporting my people

Ask for audience input

Which is just a story

Which guides our activations

MY AUDIENCE CARES ABOUT...

I wish I knew.

Being understood

My brand.

TRY AGAIN

CHECK OUT
The Two-Way Brief

CHECK OUT
How to Ignite the Fire

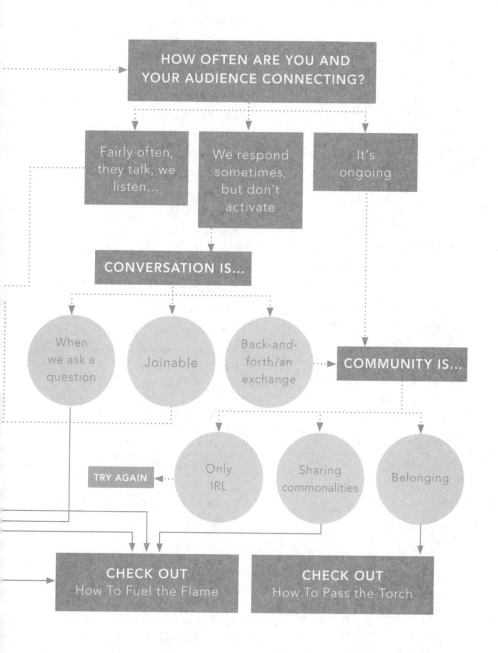

HOW OFTEN ARE YOU AND YOUR AUDIENCE CONNECTING?

- Fairly often, they talk, we listen...
- We respond sometimes, but don't activate
- It's ongoing

CONVERSATION IS...

- When we ask a question
- Joinable
- Back-and-forth/an exchange

COMMUNITY IS...

- Only IRL
- Sharing commonalities
- Belonging

TRY AGAIN

CHECK OUT
How To Fuel the Flame

CHECK OUT
How To Pass the Torch

Index

Image Reference

HQ Trivia Game: **Source:** Digiday, Day One Agency

HQ Trivia Players: **Source:** New York Post, Stefano Giovannini

Beyoncé Tweet: **Source:** Twitter, @thebeyworld

Beyoncé Run the World: **Source:** Tumblr, I Am Beyonce

Beyoncé: **Source:** Beyonce Mrs. Carter World Tour

Beyoncé Tweet: **Source:** Twitter, @BabyDollAriana

Beyoncé Tweet: **Source:** Twitter, @LaticiaD

Beyoncé Tomi Lahren: **Source:** Complex

Beyoncé Fans: **Source:** Bossip

Obsessee: **Source:** Socialix Blog

Girls Rock: **Source:** Girls Rock! Chicago

Girl Cult: **Source:** Girl Cult Festival

Shimmur: **Source:** AppShopper

Ella Victoria: **Source:** YouTube, Ella Victoria

Gen Z Female: **Source:** Shutterstock

The Art of Warfare: **Source:** TechCrunch

Boy Scouts: **Source:** Huffington Post

Whistle Sports: **Source:** Variety Magazine, Whistle Sports

CoderDojo: **Source:** ChangeX.org

Taco Bell Quesalupa: **Source:** Business Insider

Gen Z Male: **Source:** Shutterstock

Makeup (Millennial Female): **Source:** Shutterstock

bRUNch Running: **Source:** Instagram, @mountainsandmimosas

Women Who Whiskey: **Source:** LA Weekly, Ian Vergara

FemCity: **Source:** FemCity.com

Orangetheory Fitness: **Source:** Orangetheory Fitness

Millennial Female: **Source:** Adobe Stock

Minecraft: **Source:** AP Minecraft

Crossfit: **Source:** PT Educator

Saturdays Are For The Boys: **Source:** Twitter, @gibbysmallsss

Centennial 38: **Source:** Facebook, @Centennial38

Parlor Social Club: **Source:** The LA Fashion Magazine

Millennial Male: **Source:** Adobe Stock

Lean In Circles: **Source:** Lean In

WMN Space: **Source:** WMN Space

Home Decorating: **Source:** Country Living, Annie Schlechter

Family: **Source:** Shutterstock

Health: **Source:** Genius Kitchen, @dageret

Gen X Female: **Source:** Shutterstock

Entrepreneur's Organization: **Source:** Entrepreneur's Organization

Gen X Motorcycle: **Source:** Shutterstock

FanDuel: **Source:** Let's Talk Fantasy Football

Legacy Recordings: **Source:** Facebook, @LegacyRecordings

Sierra Club: **Source:** Sierra Club

Gen X Male: **Source:** Shutterstock

Red Hat Society: **Source:** Hartford Courant, Quoron Walker

Silver Sneakers: **Source:** Shutterstock

Animal Rescue: **Source:** Chelsea Rescue

Sixty and Me: **Source:** Sixty and Me

Craftsy Unlimited: **Source:** Missouri Star Quilt Company

Baby Boomer Female: **Source:** Shutterstock

AARP: **Source:** AARP, Greg Gibson

Rotary Club: **Source:** Aurora Rotary Club

PR!ME: **Source:** Sixty and Me

Motorcycles, Boomer Male: **Source:** The Oregonian

Travel, Boomer Male: **Source:** Tourist Destinations

Baby Boomer Male: **Source:** Shutterstock

Sweatcoin Opening Page: **Source:** Sweatcoin

Sweatcoin Spend, Convert, Track: **Source:** Sweatcoin

Sweatcoin Rewards: **Source:** Make Tech Easier

Southwest Rapid Rewards: **Source:** Southwest

Comic-Con: **Source:** The Mary Sue

Celebration Florida: **Source:** Zillow

Latitude Margaritaville: **Source:** Latitude Margaritaville

Johnny Cupcakes: **Source:** Startup Camp

Fat Face: **Source:** What's Up Newp

Fat Face Van: **Source:** Lineup Media

Serengetee: **Source:** Serengetee

Fernet-Branca Coins: **Source:** Tails of the Cocktail Foundation, Bret Kragerud

Fernet-Branca Drink: **Source:** Drinks Enthusiast

Disney Pin Trading Cart: **Source:** Trip Savvy

Disney Pin Trading Collection: **Source:** Collins Race 1, Elly and Caroline Collins

Christian Louboutin: **Source:** Christian Louboutin

Christian Louboutin Shoes: **Source:** the Look

Tito's Vodka Dogs: **Source:** Tito's Vodka

Tito's Vodka Sign: **Source:** Tito's Vodka

Guinness Storehouse Tourists: **Source:** Expedia, Tourism Media

Guinness Storehouse Waterfall: **Source:** Drink Me Magazine

Vans Off the Wall: **Source:** Marketing Interactive

Organic Valley: **Source:** YouTube, Organic Valley

GoPro Surfing: **Source:** Surfing Magazine, GoPro

GoPro Van: **Source:** Forbes, GoPro

Essie Nail Polish: **Source:** Essie

Jeep Tire Cover: **Source:** RT28 Motors

Jeep Wave: **Source:** Jeep Guide

In-N-Out Secret Menu: **Source:** In-N-Out

In-N-Out Double-Double: **Source:** The Food Hacker

American Eagle Studio: **Source:** Business Insider, Hollis Johnson

NikeiD: **Source:** Behance, Bob Greenberg

Freixenet Halloween: **Source:** Beverage Dynamics

Freixenet Bottles: **Source:** The Knot, Freixenet

Xbox Design Lab Controller: **Source:** Windows Central

Xbox Design Lab Options: **Source:** TechCrunch

Bar that Jack Built: **Source:** Marketing Magazine, Jack Daniel's

My Starbucks Idea: **Source:** Starbucks

Victorinox Swiss Army: **Source:** Victorinox

Sapporo 100: **Source:** Moosylvania

McDonald's McRib Finder Map: **Source:** Twitter, @McDonalds

McDonald's McRib iMessage: **Source:** Fortune

Chipotle 'Cado Crusher: **Source:** Brand Eating, Chipotle

Under Armour It Comes From Below: **Source:** Adweek

Patrón Experience: **Source:** Biz Bash, Patron

Audi Sandbox Driver: **Source:** The Webby Awards

Audi Sandbox: **Source:** Kampanje

Southwest Airlines Birthday Video: **Source:** Norty Cohen

Credit Karma: **Source:** Moosylvania

E&J Brandy: **Source:** E&J Brandy

REI Co-op Events Kayaking: **Source:** REI

Rei Co-op Events Tents: **Source:** YouTube, REI

Stella Artois Water.org: **Source:** Water.org

Sevenly: **Source:** Sevenly

Häagen-Dazs: **Source:** Brand Channel

Burger King Movember: **Source:** Burger King

The Skimm: **Source:** Twitter, @theskimm

Sephora Beauty Insider: **Source:** Sephora

Sephora Insider Cards: **Source:** Hip 2 Save

Southern Tide: **Source:** Southern Tide

Cholula Hot Sauce: **Source:** Cholula

REI Opt Outside Poster: **Source:** REI

Rei Opt Outside UGC: **Source:** Instagram, #optoutside

Sephora Beauty Consultants: **Source:** Racked, Sephora

REI Force of Nature: **Source:** REI

NYX Makeup: **Source:** NYX Makeup

Curators of Sweden: **Source:** Curators of Sweden

Honda Next Door Campaign: **Source:** Honda

Honda Next Door Garage: **Source:** Adweek, Honda

J.Crew Cast Me J.Crew: **Source:** Instagram, #castmejcrew

Kentucky Fried Chicken Tweet: **Source:** Twitter, @edgette22

Kentucky Fried Chicken Portrait: **Source:** Food and Wine, KFC

IKEA Tweet: **Source:** Twitter, @mpawlo

IKEA Identify Ad: **Source:** Thrilist, IKEA

Southwest User Generated Content: **Source:** Instagram, @southwestair via @barbarastropko

Southwest GIF Response: **Source:** Facebook, SouthwestAir

Netflix Luke's Diner: **Source:** 90.5 WESA, Sara Kovash

Craftsman Club: **Source:** The Cents'able Shoppin

Wendy's Carter Wilkerson: **Source:** Twitter, @Wendys

Wendy's Twitter: **Source:** Twitter, @carterjwm

Chacos Tan Lines: **Source:** Instagram, @mylifethroughchacos

Chacos Group: **Source:** Twitter, @chacousa

Starbursts Note: **Source:** Twitter, @EmilySelihamer

Starbursts Dress: **Source:** Facebook, Artistry and Upcycling by Emily Seilhamer

Target Wedding: **Source:** Brides, Evan Rich Photography

Taco Bell Wedding Pack: **Source:** New York Post

Taco Bell Wedding Couple: **Source:** Taco Bell

Taco Bell Senior Pictures Blonde Female: **Source:** Twitter, @verysmallpeach

Taco Bell Senior Pictures Male: **Source:** Wesley Taylor Photography

Taco Bell Senior Pictures Brunette Female: **Source:** Breece Lynne

Wawa Wedding: **Source:** Twitter, @Wawa

Circle K Wedding: **Source:** Fox 10 Phoenix, Emily Jayne Photography

Works Cited

"5 Steps for More Effective Agency Briefs (A Client's Guide)." *The Bedford Group*, bedfordgroupconsulting.com/marketing-insights/client-news-5-steps-for-more-effective-agency-briefs/.

"About America's Funniest Home Videos." *AFV*, afv.com/about-the-show/.

"About." *Curators of Sweden*, curatorsofsweden.com/about/.

Adday, Michal. "Here's Where You Can Find the McDonald's McRib." *Fortune*, Fortune, 15 Nov. 2016, fortune.com/2016/11/15/mcdonalds-mcrib-finder/.

Alcántara, Ann-Marie. "Snapchat's Ecommerce Strategy Hit a New High When It Sold Out the New Air Jordans in Minutes." *Adweek*, Adweek, 22 Feb. 2018, www.adweek.com/digital/snapchats-ecommerce-strategy-hit-a-new-high-when-it-sold-out-the-new-air-jordans-in-minutes/.

Allen, Bob. "Lady Gaga's Joanne World Tour Final Numbers: $95 Million Earned & 842,000 Tickets Sold." *Billboard*, Billboard, 15 Feb. 2018, www.billboard.com/articles/columns/chart-beat/8099986/lady-gaga-joanne-world-tour-final-numbers.

Al-Muslim, Aisha. "The Making of the Tide Ad That Scored in the Super Bowl." *The Wall Street Journal*, Dow Jones & Company, 17 June 2018, www.wsj.com/articles/the-making-of-the-tide-ad-that-scored-in-the-super-bowl-1529285099?mod=searchresults.

Alter, Kara. *Fangirling, the Economy of Getting Noticed*. Shimmur, 2017, *Fangirling, the Economy of Getting Noticed*.

"America's Original Craft Vodka." *Tito's Handmade Vodka*, www.titosvodka.com/titos-story.

Anand, Bharat. *The Content Trap A Strategist's Guide to Digital Change*. Random House, 2016.

The App That Pays You to Get Fit. sweatco.in/. Accessed 2017.

askwonder.com/. AskWonder, 2017.

Bartold, John. *Walgreen's Balance Rewards Program Shows What's Possible When Strategy Meets Technology*. 24 Apr. 2014, us.epsilon.com/a-brand-new-view/region/us/walgreens-balance-rewards-whats-possible-when-strategy-meets-technology. Accessed 2018.

Bereznak, Alyssa. *Inside the BeyHive*. 3 June 2016, www.theringer.com/2016/6/3/16042806/beyonce-beyhive-online-fan-forum-b7c7226ac16d. Accessed 3 July 2018.

Bonchek, Mark, and Cara France. "Build Your Brand as a Relationship." *Harvard Business Review*, 9 May 2016, hbr.org/2016/05/build-your-brand-as-a-relationship.

Bonchek, Mark. "Why Simple Token Will Be the Stripe of Branded Currency." *Medium*, Augmenting Humanity, 9 Nov. 2017, medium.com/@markbonchek/why-simple-token-will-be-the-stripe-of-branded-currency-b5934ea6dce8.

Brannigan, Maura. "J.Crew Cast 7 'Real People' in Its 2017 Holiday Gift Guide - and You Could Be Next." *Fashionista*, Fashionista, 7 Nov. 2017, fashionista.com/2017/11/j-crew-holiday-gift-guide-2017.

Burke, Peter J., and Michael Hogg. *Contemporary Social Psychological Theories*. Stanford University Press, 2006.

Buxton, Madeline. "At Facebook's First Communities Summit, Mark Zuckerberg Shares New Mission." *Refinery29*, Refinery29, 22 June 2017, www.refinery29.com/2017/06/160364/facebook-communities-summit-2017.

Campbell-Dollaghan, Kelsey. "Celebration, Florida: The Utopian Town That America Just Couldn't Trust." *Gizmodo*, Gizmodo.com, 21 Apr. 2014, gizmodo.com/celebration-florida-the-utopian-town-that-america-jus-1564479405.

Carmichael , Sarah Green. "How Focusing on Content Leads the Media Astray." *Harvard Business Review*, 23 Nov. 2016, hbr.org/ideacast/2016/11/how-focusing-on-content-leads-the-media-astray.

"#ChacoNation." *Chaco*, 2018, www.chacos.com/US/en/chaconation/?sma=sm.00iayrkl107eeol10vn1082ixxptm.

Chaykowski, Kathleen. "Mark Zuckerberg Gives Facebook A New Mission." *Forbes*, Forbes Magazine, 22 June 2017, www.forbes.com/sites/kathleenchaykowski/2017/06/22/mark-zuckerberg-gives-facebook-a-new-mission/.

"Cholula Teams Up With All-Star Pitcher Noah Syndergaard to Celebrate Fans and Release New Limited Edition Flavor." Multivu PR, 8 June 2017, www.multivu.com/players/English/8118351-order-of-cholula-noah-syndergaard-sweet-habanero/.

"Classic Limited Edition | Victorinox Swiss Army (USA)." *Victorinox Swiss Army*, 2018, www.swissarmy.com/us/en/Explore/Inspiration/Classic-Limited-Edition/cms/classic-limited-edition.

Cohen, David. "Mark Zuckerberg Wants Facebook to 'Bring the World Closer Together'." Adweek, Adweek, 22 June 2017, www.adweek.com/digital/mark-zuckerberg-wants-facebook-to-bring-the-world-closer-together/.

Cohen, Norty, and Eduardo Luz. "Swear Like A Mother Interview." 22 June 2018.

Cohen, Norty, and Nicole Portwood. "Tito's Vodka For Dog People Interview." 6 Dec. 2017.

Cohen, Norty. *The Participation Game*. IdeaPress Publishing, 2017.

"Conversation." *Dictionary.com*, www.dictionary.com/browse/conversation?s=t.

Costco Corporate Profile. 2018, phx.corporate-ir.net/phoenix.zhtml?c=83830&p=irol-homeprofile_pf. Accessed 2018.

CubeYou, 2017, www.cubeyou.com/.

CubeYou, 2018, www.cubeyou.com/.

Day, Patrick Kevin. "David Letterman Retires: A Brief History of the Top Ten List." *Los Angeles Times*, Los Angeles Times, 18 May 2015, www.latimes.com/entertainment/tv/showtracker/la-et-st-david-letterman-retires-history-top-ten-list-20150501-htmlstory.html.

Deis, Robert. "The First Letterman 'Top Ten' List Debuted 25 Years Ago Today..." This Day in Quotes, 2010, www.thisdayinquotes.com/2010/09/first-letterman-top-ten-list-debuted-25.html.

Design, Capsule. "Mother's Day: Uncensored – Capsule Design – Medium." *Medium*, Augmenting Humanity, 3 July 2017, medium.com/@capsuledesign/mothers-day-uncensored-583f70462d4f.

Donnelly, Gordon. "75 Super-Useful Facebook Statistics for 2018." *WordStream*, 26 June 2018, www.wordstream.com/blog/ws/2017/11/07/facebook-statistics.

Drake, Bruce. "6 New Findings about Millennials." *Pew Research Center*, Pew Research Center, 7 Mar. 2014, www.pewresearch.org/fact-tank/2014/03/07/6-new-findings-about-millennials/.

Duggan, Bill. "Client/ Agency Relationships: It's All in the Brief – Why ANA Wants to Help." *The Drum*, Cognition, 29 Apr. 2015, www.thedrum.com/opinion/2015/04/29/client-agency-relationships-its-all-brief-why-ana-wants-help-clean-garbage.

Earle, Johnny. "About." *Johnny Cupcakes*, 2018, johnnycupcakes.com/pages/about.

Edgecomb, Carolyn. "Social Media Marketing: The Importance of a Two-Way Conversation." *IMPACT: Inbound Marketing Strategy, Advice, and Agency,* 27 Mar. 2017, www.impactbnd.com/blog/social-media-marketing-the-importance-of-a-two-way-conversation.

Elber, Lynn. "Sylvester 'Pat' Weaver Dies." *The Washington Post,* WP Company, 18 Mar. 2002, www.washingtonpost.com/archive/local/2002/03/18/sylvester-pat-weaver-dies/a7e55c6a-f2b1-4e2f-a470-b848ae48fbf8/?utm_term=.ee21d38d8c7f.

"Embracing the Power of Superfans and Social Media." *Adweek,* Adweek, 26 Apr. 2016, www.adweek.com/digital/geoff-smith-crowdtwist-guest-post-superfans/.

"Emirates Loyalty Program Skywards Reaches 20 Million Members." *BusinessClass,* 28 Feb. 2018, www.businessclass.co.uk/emirates-skywards-reached-20-million-members/.

Fahey, Mike. "I Made A Controller Using Xbox Design Lab's New Colors And Parts." *Kotaku,* Kotaku.com, 29 June 2017, kotaku.com/i-made-a-controller-using-xbox-design-labs-new-options-1796519820.

Feldman, Jamie. "You Need To See This Dress Made Out Of 10,000 Starburst Wrappers." *The Huffington Post,* 18 May 2017, www.huffingtonpost.com/entry/starburst-wrapper-dress_us_591d6f1ce4b034684b098dd3.

Fournier, Susan, and Lara Lee. "Getting Brand Communities Right." *Harvard Business Review,* Apr. 2009, hbr.org/2009/04/getting-brand-communities-right.

Fox 10 Staff. "Valley Couple Takes Wedding Photos at Circle K." *Fox 5,* 23 Sept. 2016, www.fox5ny.com/news/valley-couple-takes-wedding-photos-at-circle-k.

Fraade-Blanar, Zoe, and Aaron M. Glazer. *Superfandom: How Our Obsessions Are Changing What We Buy and Who We Are.* W.W. Norton & Company, 2017.

"Freixenet Wine Halloween Campaign Embraces Customization, Costumes." *Beverage Dynamics,* 22 Oct. 2015, beveragedynamics.com/2015/10/22/freixenet-wine-halloween-campaign-embraces-customization-costumes/.

Fulton, Wil. "Wawa vs. Sheetz: Behind the Most Heated Food Rivalry in the Country." *Thrillist,* Thrillist, 27 Mar. 2017, www.thrillist.com/eat/nation/wawa-vs-sheetz-gas-station-food.

Garcia, Tonya. "Chipotle Launches Online Avocado Game, ''Cado Crusher'." *MarketWatch,* MarketWatch, 24 Jan. 2017, www.marketwatch.com/story/chipotle-launches-online-avocado-game-cado-crusher-2017-01-24.

Giovannini, Stefano. "New York Post." New York Post, 10 Jan. 2018, nypost.com/2018/01/10/inside-the-latest-millennial-obsession-hq-trivia/.

Godin, Seth. *Tribes: We Need You to Lead Us.* Piatkus, 2010.

González, Ángel. 'As the REI Outdoor Gear Co-Op Thrives, Does It Have Members or Merely Shoppers?' 31 May 2016, www.adn.com/business/article/rei-thrives-does-it-have-members-or-merely-shoppers/2016/02/05/. Accessed 2018.

Gots, Jason. "Your Storytelling Brain." Big Think, Big Think Inc., 15 Jan. 2012, bigthink.com/overthinking-everything-with-jason-gots/your-storytelling-brain.

Grant, Adam, and Sheryl Sandberg. Originals How Non-Conformists Move the World. Penguin Publishing Group, 2017.

Grant, John. *The Brand Innovation Manifesto: How to Build Brands, Redefine Markets and Defy Conventions.* John Wiley, 2007.

Green, Dennis, and Hollis Johnson. "American Eagle Just Opened a Store of the Future Complete with Free Laundry Machines and an IPad in Every Dressing Room." *Business Insider*, Business Insider, 14 Nov. 2017, www.businessinsider.com/american-eagle-store-free-laundry-nyc-2017-11.

Greene, Sydney C. "Couple Gets Married at Taco Bell in Las Vegas." *USA Today*, Gannett Satellite Information Network, 28 June 2017, www.usatoday.com/story/news/nation-now/2017/06/28/couple-gets-married-taco-bell-las-vegas-cantina/434899001/.

Greenwood, Shannon, et al. "Social Media Update 2016." *Pew Research Center: Internet, Science & Tech*, 11 Nov. 2016, www.pewinternet.org/2016/11/11/social-media-update-2016/.

Griner, David. "KFC Painted a Portrait for the Man Who Spotted Its 11 Herbs and Spices Stunt on Twitter." *Adweek*, Adweek, 8 Nov. 2017, www.adweek.com/creativity/kfc-painted-a-portrait-for-the-man-who-spotted-its-11-herbs-and-spices-stunt-on-twitter/.

Guinness Storehouse, 2018, www.guinness-storehouse.com/en/ground-floor.

Handley, Lucy. "These Are the Commercials That Won the Super Bowl in 2018 - and Here's How Much They Cost." *CNBC*, CNBC, 6 Feb. 2018, www.cnbc.com/2018/02/05/super-bowl-2018-the-best-tv-commercials-and-how-much-they-cost.html.

Hatic, Dana. "Drink Free Coffee Like a Gilmore Girl at Hundreds of Luke's Diner Pop-Ups Across America." *Eater*, Eater, 3 Oct. 2016, www.eater.com/2016/10/3/12929778/gilmore-girls-netflix-lukes-diner-coffee-california-new-york-canada.

Hetrick, Matt. "A Southern Tide Case Study." *MattHetrick*, Wordpress, 7 May 2012, matthetrick1.wordpress.com/2012/05/07/a-southern-tide-case-study/.

Hines, Nick. "The Secret Bartender Handshake You Never Knew Existed." *VinePair*, 26 Apr. 2017, vinepair.com/articles/the-secret-bartender-handshake-you-never-knew-existed/.

"History of the GoPro | Nick Woodman's Story | GP Buyer's Guide." *Cam Authority*, 2016, www.goprobuyersguide.com/story/.

"History." *Vans USA*, 2018, www.vans.com/history.html.

Horoszowski, Mark. "'Purpose' Is the Key to Engaging Millennials in Volunteering and Giving." *The Huffington Post*, 3 May 2016, www.huffingtonpost.com/mark-horoszowski/purpose-is-the-key-to-eng_b_9824326.html.

"How Craftsman Hammered, Sawed and Built an Online Community for Makers." Livefyre, 2016.

"How We Work." *Sevenly*, www.sevenly.org/pages/how-we-work.

"IHG® Challenges Brands to Address the Needs of the Uncompromising Customer in the 'Age of I.'" *InterContinental Hotels Group PLC*, 16 Jan. 2017, www.ihgplc.com/news-and-media/news-releases/2017/ihg-challenges-brands-to-address-the-needs-of-the-uncompromising-customer-in-the-age-of-i.

"IKEA FAMILY: A Resource for Sustainable Living." *Context Partners*, 207AD, staging. contextpartners.com/portfolio/ikea-family-loyalty-program-engagement/.

Jardine, Alexandra. "Honda Campaign via Sid Lee Turns Owners' Garages into Pop-up Dealerships in France." *AdAge*, AdAge, 30 Oct. 2017, creativity-online.com/work/honda-the-honda-next-door/53109.

"Jeep Wave Rules - Here's Who Waves First, Who Waves & Who Doesn't, And How To Do The Official Jeep Hand Wave Every Time You Pass Another Jeep | The Jeep Guide." *Jeep Guide*, The Fun Times Guide to Jeeping, 5 May 2018, jeeps.thefuntimesguide.com/jeep _wave/.

Johnson, Lauren. "HQ Trivia Is Dictating When and How Consumers Use Apps and Inspiring a Host of Imitators." – *Adweek*, Adweek, 5 Mar. 2018, www.adweek.com/digital/how-hq-trivia-is-inspiring-a-new-on-demand-viewing-model-for-apps/.

Kapler, Jason. "Shifting From One-Way Broadcast to Two-Way Dialog Changes Everything." *Adweek*, Adweek, 10 Apr. 2017, www.adweek.com/digital/shifting-from-one-way-broadcast-to-two-way-dialog-changes-everything/.

Kelly, Heather. *Jeff Bezos Reveals Amazon Has More than 100 Million Prime Members.* 19 Apr. 2018, money.cnn.com/2018/04/18/technology/amazon-100-million-prime-members/index.html. Accessed 2018.

Kemp-Robertson, Paul, director. *Bitcoin. Sweat. Tide. Meet the Future of Branded Currency.* June 2013, www.ted.com/talks/paul_kemp_robertson_bitcoin_sweat_tide_meet_the_ future_of_branded_currency. Accessed 2017.

Kepley, Vance. "The Museum of Broadcast Communications - Encyclopedia of Television - Weaver, Sylvester (Pat)." *The Museum of Broadcast Communications - Encyclopedia of Television* - Vietnam on Television, www.museum.tv/eotv/weaversylve.htm.

Kerridge, Kevin. *5 Viral Marketing Techniques You Can Learn From HQ Trivia.* 30 Jan. 2018, www.inc.com/kevin-kerridge/5-lessons-marketers-can-learn-from-hq-trivias-viral-success. html. Accessed 3 July 2018.

Knuffman, Krista. "Great Questions LLC." Missouri, St Louis, 2017.

Koltun, Natalie. "Kraft Encourages Moms to 'Swear like a Mother' in Viral Campaign." *Marketing Dive*, Industry Dive, 8 May 2017, www.marketingdive.com/news/kraft-encourages-moms-to-swear-like-a-mother-in-viral-campaign/442166/.

"Kraft Macaroni & Cheese - 'Swear Like A Mother.'" *YouTube*, YouTube, 3 Jan. 2018, www.youtube.com/watch?v=sgBVrEb_qXY.

Lachel, Christian. "Brand Homes Create Brand Super Fans." *Campaign US*, 3 July 2017, www.campaignlive.com/article/brand-homes-create-brand-super-fans/1438249.

Leff, Gary. "Marriott Reaches 100 Million Loyalty Members, Introduces Experience Bookings." *View from the Wing*, Boarding Area, 21 Mar. 2017, viewfromthewing boardingarea.com/2017/03/21/marriott-reaches-100-million-loyalty-members-introduces-experience-bookings/.

Lester, Tracey Lomrantz. "The True Story Of How Christian Louboutin Shoes Got Those Trademark Red Soles." *Glamour*, Glamour Magazine, 21 Mar. 2011, www.glamour.com/ story/the-true-story-of-how-christia.

Machado, Fernando. "WorldWide Partners Miami Summit, 2018 ."

"Make It Right, Swear Like a Mother - The Shorty Awards." *The Shorty Awards - Honoring the Best of Social Media*, 2018, shortyawards.com/10th/make-it-right-swear-like-a-mother.

"Malcolm Gladwell Teaches Writing." Performance by Malcolm Gladwell, *Masterclass, 2018,* www.masterclass.com/classes/malcolm-gladwell-teaches-writing.

Manners, Tim. "Shopper Stories." New York, New York City, 2017.

Marcario, Rose. *Patagonia CEO Explains Why They're Suing Donald Trump*. 6 Dec. 2017, time.com/5052617/patagonia-ceo-suing-donald-trump/. Accessed 2018.

McEachern, Alex. "Loyalty Case Study: Sephora's Beauty Insider (VIB)." *Smile.io*, 28 July 2017, blog.smile.io/loyalty-case-study-sephoras-beauty-insider-vib.

Meola, Andrew. "Starbucks' Loyalty Program Now Holds More Money than Some Banks." *Business Insider*, Business Insider, 13 June 2016, www.businessinsider.com/starbucks-loyalty-program-now-holds-more-money-than-some-banks-2016-6.

Miller, Jeff. "In-N-Out's Secret Menu, Ranked." *Thrillist*, Thrillist, 19 Aug. 2015, www.thrillist.com/eat/los-angeles/the-in-n-out-secret-menu-ranked.

Monllos, Kristina. "This Snapchat Game From Under Armour Turns You Into Cam Newton and Makes You Dodge Wolves." *Adweek*, Adweek, 27 Sept. 2016, www.adweek.com/brand-marketing/snapchat-game-under-armour-turns-you-cam-newton-and-makes-you-dodge-wolves-173743/.

Morris, Chris. "Here's How Many People Participated in Women's Marches This Year." *Fortune*, Fortune, 22 Jan. 2018, fortune.com/2018/01/22/womens-march-2018-numbers/.

Mundahl, Erin. "Facebook Offers Sense of Belonging for Wary Millennials." *St. Cloud Times*, SCTimes, 21 Mar. 2015, www.sctimes.com/story/opinion/2015/03/21/facebook-offers-sense-belonging-wary-millennials/25056327/.

"My Starbucks Idea: Crowdsourcing for Customer Satisfaction and Innovation." *Digital Innovation and Transformation*, Harvard Business School, 31 Oct. 2015, digit.hbs.org/submission/my-starbucks-idea-crowdsourcing-for-customer-satisfaction-and-innovation/.

Nafarrete, Jonathan. "Audi Creates VR Sandbox Track You Can Shape And Drive Yourself." *VRScout*, 22 Feb. 2017, vrscout.com/news/audi-vr-sandbox-track-shape-drive/.

Noonan, Keith. "5 Things GameStop Management Wants You to Know." *The Motley Fool*, The Motley Fool, 11 Sept. 2017, www.fool.com/investing/2017/09/11/5-things-gamestop-management-wants-you-to-know.aspx.

Nudd, Tim. "Ikea Had a Great Reaction to Balenciaga Making a $2,145 Version of Its 99-Cent Blue Bag." *Adweek*, Adweek, 25 Apr. 2017, www.adweek.com/agencies/ikea-had-a-great-reaction-to-balenciaga-making-a-2145-version-of-its-iconic-99-cent-blue-bag/.

Nudd, Tim. "Inside Year Three of #OptOutside With REI's Chief Creative Officer." *Adweek*, Adweek, 20 Nov. 2017, www.adweek.com/creativity/inside-year-three-of-optoutside-with-reis-chief-creative-officer/.

Nudd, Tim. "The King Shaved His Mustache for the First Time for Burger King's Movember Campaign." *Adweek*, Adweek, 1 Nov. 2017, www.adweek.com/creativity/the-king-shaved-his-mustache-for-the-first-time-for-burger-kings-movember-campaign/.

Nussbaum, Rachel. "Sephora Cast 10 of Its Own Employees in Its Most Diverse Campaign Yet." *Glamour*, Glamour Magazine, 31 Oct. 2017, www.glamour.com/story/sephora-holiday-ad-diversity.

Ong, Thuy. "Facebook Gives Super-Fans a Home with New Groups Feature." *The Verge*, The Verge, 20 July 2017, www.theverge.com/2017/7/20/16002616/facebook-groups-feature-pages-administrators.

Onorato, Amy. "5 Ways HQ Nails Mobile Audience Engagement." *DMN*, 13 Mar. 2018, www.dmnews.com/channel-marketing/mobile/article/13034650/5-ways-hq-nails-mobile-audience-engagement.

Oster, Erik. "New Study Finds That Agencies and Marketers Are Still at Odds in 2017." *Adweek,* Adweek, 20 Jan. 2017, www.adweek.com/brand-marketing/new-study-finds-agencies-and-marketers-are-still-odds-2017-175631/.

Oster, Erik. "Stella Artois Teams With Matt Damon and Water.org for First Super Bowl Appearance Since 2011." *Adweek,* Adweek, 16 Jan. 2018, www.adweek.com/brand-marketing/stella-artois-teams-with-matt-damon-and-water-org-for-first-super-bowl-appearance-since-2011/.

"Our Humble History | *Organic Valley.*" Organic Valley, www.organicvalley.coop/about-us/our-humble-history/.

"Outdoor Classes, Events & Outings." *REI Co-Op Journal,* REI, www.rei.com/events.

"Patrón Tequila Unveils 'The Patrón Experience,' One of the First Brands to Create a Hand-Held Augmented Reality Innovation." *PR Newswire,* PRNewswire, 20 Sept. 2017, www.prnewswire.com/news-releases/patron-tequila-unveils-the-patron-experience-one-of-the-first-brands-to-create-a-hand-held-augmented-reality-innovation-300522885.html.

Perez, Sarah. "Ex-Apple Execs Take on Twitch with Launch of New Social Broadcasting Platform Caffeine." *TechCrunch,* Tech Network, 31 Jan. 2018, techcrunch.com/2018/01/31/ex-apple-execs-take-on-twitch-with-launch-of-new-social-broadcasting-platform-caffeine/.

Perkins, Neil. "IPA Future of Agencies Systems and Empathy." Institute of Practitioners of Advertising , Mar. 2017.

Petski, Denise. "'Gordon Ramsay's 24 Hours To Hell And Back' Renewed For Second Season By Fox." Deadline, Deadline, 27 June 2018, deadline.com/2018/06/gordon-ramsays-24-hours-to-hell-and-back-renewed-second-season-fox-1202418213/.

Pham, Tam. "Why Building Community Is the New 'Growth Hack.'" *The Hustle,* 10 Feb. 2016, thehustle.co/why-building-community-is-the-new-growth-hack.

Probst, Emmanuel. "Aligning Brand Strategy And Influencer Marketing." *Branding Strategy Insider,* 4 Aug. 2017, www.brandingstrategyinsider.com/2017/08/aligning-brand-strategy-and-influencer-marketing.html?utm_source=feedburner.

Puhak, Janine. "Couple Takes Wedding Photos at Target." *Fox News,* FOX News Network, 3 Mar. 2018, www.foxnews.com/lifestyle/2018/03/03/couple-takes-wedding-photos-at-target.html.

Richards, Katie. "Moms Admit to Swearing in Front of Their Kids, and Kraft Mac and Cheese Is Totally Chill About It." *Adweek,* Adweek, 3 May 2017, www.adweek.com brand-marketing/moms-admit-to-swearing-in-front-of-their-kids-and-kraft-mac-and-cheese-is-totally-chill-about-it/.

Rolfsmeier, Liz. "Senior Motorcycle Enthusiasts Ride Together from Lakeville's Heritage Center." *Star Tribune,* Star Tribune, 22 Aug. 2015, www.startribune.com/senior-motorcycle-enthusiasts-ride-together-from-lakeville-s-heritage-center/322560551/.

Sandstrom, Aleksandra, and Becka A. Alper. "If the U.S. Had 100 People: Charting Americans' Religious Beliefs and Practices." *Pew Research Center,* Pew Research Center, 1 Dec. 2016, www.pewresearch.org/fact-tank/2016/12/01/if-the-u-s-had-100-people-charting-americans-religious-beliefs-and-practices/.

Schlangenstein, Mary. 'American Airlines Has the Industry's Largest Loyalty Program.' 24 Mar. 2015, skift.com/2015/03/24/american-airlines-now-has-the-industrys-largest-loyalty-program/. Accessed 2018.

Schumaker, Erin. "The Complicated Psychology Of Sports Superfandom." *The Huffington Post,* 15 May 2015, www.huffingtonpost.com/2015/04/08/super-fan-psychology_n_7012324.html.

Shu, Catherine. "NYX Cosmetics, Known for Its 'Digital-First' Marketing Strategy, Launches Its Own App." *TechCrunch,* TechCrunch, 14 Sept. 2017, techcrunch.com/2017/09/14/nyx-makeup-crew/.

Smiley, Minda. "No Super Bowl for You: Why Some Brands Aren't Buying Spots in This Year's Game." *The Drum,* Cognition, 29 Jan. 2018, www.thedrum.com/news/2018/01/29/no-super-bowl-you-why-some-brands-aren-t-buying-spots-year-s-game.

Smith, Geoff. "Study: Millennials Are the Most Brand-Loyal Generation." *Inc.com,* Inc., 30 Sept. 2015, www.inc.com/geoff-smith/millennials-becoming-more-loyal-in-era-of-consumer-choice.html.

Southwest Rapid Rewards. "Happy Birthday!" Received by Norty Cohen, *Happy Birthday!,* 25 Nov. 2017.

Sprout Social, 2016.

Sprout Social, 2017.

Sprout Social, 2018.

Sprout Social. "Sprout Social Index 2018." Sprout Social, 2018.

Steitz, Jeff, and Ryan Westberg. "Mission." *Serengetee,* www.serengetee.com/men-women/mission/.

Stern, Matthew. "Segmentation Is Central to Nike's Success." *RetailWire,* 22 Mar. 2018, www.retailwire.com/discussion/segmentation-is-central-to-nikes-success/.

Stitzinger, Jennie. "Häagen-Dazs Loves Honey Bees." *Bee Informed Partnership,* 19 Mar. 2012, beeinformed.org/2012/03/19/3651/.

"The Story | FatFace.com." *FatFace US,* 2018, us.fatface.com/about-fatface/the-story.html.

Strickland, Cara. "The Legend and Lore of the Fernet-Branca Challenge Coins." *Tales of the Cocktail,* 27 Feb. 2017, talesofthecocktail.com/history/part-family-behind-scenes-fernet-branca-challenge-coins.

Stritzke, Jerry. "Force of Nature: Let's Level the Playing Field." *REI Co-Op Journal,* REI, 2 Apr. 2017, www.rei.com/blog/news/force-of-nature-lets-level-the-playing-field.

Strutner, Suzy. "Teen's Senior Portraits Were Shot In Taco Bell, And They're Perfect." *The Huffington Post,* 24 May 2017, www.huffingtonpost.com/entry/taco-bell-senior-portraits_us_5925c86de4b0650cc0213ed2.

Taylor, Glenn. "Communities Influence The Next Wave Of Customer Engagement Strategies - Retail TouchPoints." *Retail TouchPoints,* 12 Apr. 2016, www.retailtouchpoints.com/features/trend-watch/communities-influence-the-next-wave-of-customer-engagement-strategies.

TedxTalks. Primal Branding. Performance by Patrick Hanlon, *YouTube,* TEDxElPaso, 7 Nov. 2016, www.youtube.com/watch?v=7JAFocvQ91Q.

Thompson, Anne Bahr. *Do Good: Embracing Brand Citizenship to Fuel Both Purpose and Profit.* AMACOM, American Management Association, 2018.

"Ultimate Guide to Disney Pin Trading." *Disney Dose,* 5 July 2016, disneydose.com/guide-disney-pin-trading/.

Victor, Daniel. "Step Aside, Ellen DeGeneres: The New Retweet Champion Is a Nugget-Hungry Teenager." *The New York Times,* The New York Times, 9 May 2017, www.nytimes.com/2017/05/09/technology/wendys-nuggets-twitter.html.

Weaver, Pat, and Thomas M. Coffey. *The Best Seat in the House: the Golden Years of Radio and Television.* Knopf, 1994.

Weaver, Pat. "Pat Weaver Recalls The Early Fight For Tv Power." *Tribunedigital-Chicagotribune,* Chicago Tribune , 30 Jan. 1994, articles.chicagotribune.com/1994-01-30/entertainment/9401300026_1_weaver-returns-jack-benny-sylvester-pat-weaver.

Wischhover, Cheryl. "Ever Wonder How Nail Polish Gets Named? Essie Weingarten (Yes, That Essie) Reveals Her Secrets." *Fashionista,* Fashionista, 18 Apr. 2011, fashionista.com/2011/04/ever-wonder-how-nail-polish-gets-named-essie-weingarten-yes-that-essie-reveals-her-secrets.

Wong, Danny. "NikeID Makes $100M+: Co-Creation Isn't Just a Trend." *The Huffington Post,* TheHuffingtonPost.com, 25 May 2011, www.huffingtonpost.com/danny-wong/nikeid-makes-100m-co-crea_b_652214.html.

"Working for Jack: 'The Bar That Jack Built'." *Marketing Magazine,* 3 Dec. 2015, www.marketingmag.com.au/hubs-c/working-jack-bar-jack-built/.

"Worldwide Partner Conference 2015."

"Your New Home In Paradise." *Latitude Margaritaville,* www.latitudemargaritaville.com/.

Zappos. "Your Zappos.com Order." Received by Norty Cohen, *Your Zappos.com Order,* 10 July 2017.